COLM 'GOOCH'
COOPER

Photograph by Shane Cahill

DONNY MAHONEY is a writer and journalist. He was born in America and has lived in Ireland since 2004. He is one of the co-founders of the website Balls.ie, where he works today.

COLM "GOOCH" COOPER

DONNY MAHONEY

THE O'BRIEN PRESS
DUBLIN

First published 2019 by
The O'Brien Press Ltd,
12 Terenure Road East, Rathgar,
Dublin 6, D06 HD27 Ireland.
Tel: +353 1 4923333; Fax: +353 1 4922777
E-mail: books@obrien.ie.
Website: www.obrien.ie.
The O'Brien Press is a member of Publishing Ireland

ISBN: 978-1-78849-085-6

9 8 7 6 5 4 3 2 1
23 22 21 20 19

Printed and bound in Great Britain by Clays Ltd, Elcograf S.p.A.
The paper in this book is produced using pulp from managed forests.

Published in:

DUBLIN
UNESCO
City of Literature

CONTENTS

CHAPTER I

COLM'S FIRST TRAINING SESSION

On a brisk autumn morning in 1989, a freckle-faced six-year-old from Killarney left his home for his first-ever GAA training session. His name was Colm Cooper. He was heading to his GAA club Dr Crokes with his dad Mike. Colm was over the moon with excitement. He was about to take part in an U8 GAA blitz.

It was a chilly morning, but Colm wore the black and amber kit of Dr Crokes with pride. He'd been visiting the club since he learned to walk, but it was his first time wearing the Dr Crokes jersey out of the house. His four older brothers all owned the exact same kit. New kits had such an amazing smell when they came out of the plastic. He'd muck it all up soon but for now everything in the world was perfect.

'Are you nervous, Colm?' his dad asked.

'No, Dad,' Colm said. 'I just can't wait to play.'

Colm was a wispy redhead. He was the youngest in a family of seven kids. He had four older brothers Danny, Mark, Mike and Vince, and two older sisters, Geraldine and Karen. It was hard being the youngest kid – you were the last one to experience everything – but Colm was delighted his day with Dr Crokes had finally come.

'Enjoy yourself today, Colm,' his mam had said when he was leaving the house. She gave him a big hug, which made Colm squirm a bit. She had packed his gym bag with everything he'd need: his Adidas boots, a water bottle, a few bananas and some sliced oranges, and a cap in case it rained. Under his arm, he carried his most important possession in the world: a Gaelic football.

It was only a five-minute drive from their estate, which was called Ardshanavooly, to the Dr Crokes club, down on the Lewis Road. The Coopers lived in one of the biggest towns in the most beautiful county in Ireland. Dr Crokes was already Colm's home away from home. He was there all the time to watch his brothers play. Finally it was his turn.

Colm's dad wasn't from Killarney but he was a proud member of Dr Crokes. And of course, he was a very proud Kerryman. His dad knew everything about the GAA. And he knew EVERYTHING about Kerry football.

'How do you become a Kerry footballer, Dad?' Colm asked, as they pulled out of the estate.

'You practise, son!'

Colm laughed.

'No, really Dad!' he said. 'How do they pick the Kerry football team?'

'Well it starts with club,' Colm's dad said. 'First you build a reputation up at underage level, so that the selectors know you. Then when you're seventeen you might get called into the Kerry minor panel. And it snowballs from there. U21s, training squads and the like. Only the best of the best play for Kerry.'

'I want to play for Kerry some day,' Colm said.

'Well that's the beauty of it,' Colm's dad said. 'If you were born in Sligo or Timbuktu, it wouldn't be an option. But you were born a Kerryman. And that green and gold jersey is one of the many privileges that comes with being from here.'

They pulled up in front of the gates of the club. Colm could see a group of kids his age gathering on the main pitch.

'One thing to keep in mind, Colm, is that all of the Kerry greats, the likes of Pat Spillane and Bomber Liston, all learned their trade with their club. And when their careers with Kerry ended, they went back to their club. Club is everything.'

Colm understood.

'Go on and join the other lads.'

'Bye, Dad!'

Colm ran from the car and joined in the blitz. Coach Pádraig O'Shea was there to guide them through some drills. How to hand pass. How to solo. How to pick the ball up off the ground with your foot. Colm loved every second of it. An hour passed in the blink of an eye.

'Before we wrap it up, we're going to give everyone a chance of kicking a penalty against a real goalie,' one of the trainers announced.

Coach Peter, goalie for the Dr Crokes senior team, stood between the posts in his goalie's kit.

He was a real character. He had a thick moustache and loved telling jokes. Like Colm, he was from Ardshanavooly.

Eventually it was Colm's turn to take his penalty. He placed the ball on the spot and stood over the ball.

'What's your name, son?' Coach Peter said.

'I'm Colm Cooper from Ardshan,' Colm replied.

'Ah another one of the Coopers of Ardshanavooly,' Coach Peter. 'A fine footballing family you have there.'

All of a sudden, Coach Peter gave him a funny look.

'Do you know what you remind me of, young Cooper?' Coach Peter said.

'No,' Colm said.

'Do you know those Goochie dolls that they're selling in the shops?'

All the kids laughed. At the time there was a very popular kids doll in Kerry named Goochie. The Goochie doll had big, bright red hair, like Bosco.

Colm blushed.

'You're a bit like a Goochie doll with that red hair you've got. Now let's see if you can put a penalty past me, Goochie.'

Colm was determined to score a goal. On every football, there's one perfect spot and Colm tried to find it. He struck the ball sweetly, firing it into the bottom right corner. Coach Peter dove, but couldn't stop the shot.

'Great penalty, Gooch!' Coach Peter shouted, as he picked himself up off the ground. Colm pumped his fist. He was the only player to score his penalty. It was his first experience of scoring a goal on a Gaelic football pitch. What a feeling it was!

CHAPTER 2

ITALIA 90 FEVER SWEEPS KILLARNEY

Colm and all his brothers were on the Ardshan front green, kicking a soccer ball around. They were about to start a game of soccer with ten of their neighbours. Later that June afternoon, Ireland would be playing Romania in the World Cup Round of 16.

Italia 90 fever had swept Ardshanavooly. It was Ireland's first-ever World Cup. The estate had two areas for playing sport – the front green and the back green – and soccer was the only game being played in Ardshan that summer. Colm was seven years old. He'd never experienced anything like it.

The whole country had gone soccer-mad.

Colm was the smallest kid in this soccer match. The lads in the estate – especially his own brothers – were so competitive when it came to sport. They treated every game of soccer like it was the actual World Cup.

Colm's brothers Mark and Vince were the captains. They went through all the lads until Colm was the only one who hadn't been chosen.

'C'mon Colm you're with us,' Vince said.

'Why did you pick me last?' Colm said to Vince. 'I'm better some of these lads.'

'Don't take it personally,' Vince said. 'You're the youngest of anyone here.'

It was the first summer that his brothers let him play in their soccer games.

'You're too small,' they used to say.

But Colm was getting better at soccer. Even if he was just seven years old, Colm was more skilful on the ball than some of his neighbours like Paddy or Niall, lads who were almost twelve years old. Colm knew he would have to prove to them how good he was. He didn't mind.

The two teams lined up across the green. The

pitch on the Ardshan green was makeshift. There were no lines. There were no markings. They used jumpers for goals. But in the imagination of all the Ardshan kids, the front green was like the Stadio Olimpico in Rome, with 100,000 people in the terraces going mad.

'We're Ireland!' Mark shouted.

'No, we're Ireland!' Vince shouted back.

All that summer, Colm and the kids on the green had spent days and night pretending they were the Boys In Green and singing about the Ireland team and their coach Jack Charlton:

'We're all part of Jackie's army, we're all off to Italy. And we'll really shake them up when we win the World Cup because Ireland are the greatest football team!'

Gaelic football was Colm's favourite sport, but he also loved playing soccer with the other kids in the estate. He loved having the ball at his feet. When he played he wanted to be like John Barnes, the England striker who played with his favourite club, Liverpool.

The game kicked off. Colm stole the ball from his brother Mark. He dribbled past one player, then nutmegged another. He was clear on goal and about to shoot when ... *thwack* ... Mark came in and slide-tackled him from behind.

'Fair tackle,' Mark shouted. 'I got the ball first!'

Maybe it was a fair tackle, but it was also very painful. Colm's ankle was bruised and really sore. He felt like crying, but if he did, he knew they wouldn't let him play anymore.

Vince gave him a hand up.

'You need to see those challenges coming, Colm,' Vince said. 'Otherwise you'll end up with two broken ankles!'

Colm nodded and dusted himself off. He'd have to be tougher and smarter if he wanted to play with the bigger kids.

Colm's mother stuck her head out the front door.

'Lads, it's nearly kickoff. The anthems are on.'

With that, the game stopped immediately and everyone sprinted for their own house to watch the match.

Colm and all of his brothers spread themselves around the sitting room. Their parents and two sisters were already watching the match. They arrived back as *Amhrán na bFhiann* was being played.

'C'mon Ireland!' they all shouted.

It was a different than watching a Gaelic football match on TV. It was slow and so tense.

'Pretty much everyone in Ireland is watching this match,' Karen said. 'Imagine.'

Romania wore bright yellow jerseys and had lots of skilled footballers, but the Irish defence was impossible to break down.

It was scoreless at half-time. It was scoreless at fulltime.

'This is going to penalties, isn't it?' Colm's dad said.

He was right. Colm's sister Geraldine had to leave the sitting room, she was too nervous. Both countries made their first four penalty kicks. Colm's mam started to pray the rosary in the other room.

Timofte, a Romanian, took the fifth, but it was saved by Bonner! David O'Leary stood over the penalty to win the match for Ireland.

'A nation holds its breath... Yes! Ireland are through to the quarterfinals of the World Cup!'

All the Coopers jumped up and hugged each other in the middle of the sitting room. Colm couldn't remember a time when he had seen his family so happy.

'Let's go for a spin!' Colm's dad said after the post-match interviews were over.

All seven Cooper kids piled into the family car. Everyone was driving around Killarney honking their horns. People were sticking out of car boots and sun roofs and car windows, screaming *'Ireland! Ireland!'* and waving Irish flags.

At the Ballydowney roundabout, people were jumping up and dancing, waving the tricolour.

'This is the power of sport, kids,' Colm's dad said. 'Remember the feeling because Ireland might not be in many more World Cups!'

Colm wondered what it must be like for the Ireland players. It must be such an amazing feeling, Colm thought, to be on the pitch today. With the whole world watching, those boys in green delivered.

CHAPTER 3

COLM'S FIRST MUNSTER FINAL

Colm woke up, giddy with excitement. It was the day of the 1991 Munster final day in Killarney and Colm's dad was bringing the whole family up the road to Fitzgerald Stadium to watch Kerry take on Limerick. Colm was eight and it was his first Munster final.

There was magic in the air in Killarney ahead of a Munster final. Colm's dad had hung the Kerry flag outside their front door and tied some green and gold streamers to the antennae of their car.

Colm went to The Mercy National School in Killarney, just like all of his brothers and sisters before him. He liked reading and writing and Irish history, but he couldn't wait for summer to roll around. It meant he could play sport for the entire day.

Summers in Ardshan were all about sport. There was nothing worse than being stuck indoors. He'd play anything and everything with his brothers and his friends from the estate. There were games of soccer on the green. They'd play rounders if they could find a bat. There was a pitch and putt course over the wall of the estate. There were tennis courts at the hotel nearby.

Every day was like the Olympics. When it rained – which it often did – there was only one thing to do: watch the *Kerry's Golden Years* video.

For Colm and his brothers, the video was the most sacred thing in their house. Kerry's eight great All-Ireland wins from 1975-1986 were captured on the two-hour long video.

Colm had easily watched the video one thousand times with his brothers. They'd all memorised the commentary of the famous goals. They'd re-enact the goals any time out on the Ardshan green.

Everywhere he went, he brought his Gaelic football with him. That summer, Colm had been telling everyone in Ardshanavooly that someday he was going to score the winning goal for Kerry in the All-Ireland final.

He told his brothers.

'You have a long way to go before you become the best footballer in this house, let alone Kerry,' Mark joked.

He told the older kids in the estate.

'A little runt like you? Playing for Kerry?' they laughed.

He told his mother and father.

'Good man Colm,' his father said.

'It's good to dream big, Colm, but you need to stay humble. You'll get nowhere in life without hard work,' she said.

Colm knew his mam was right. She was always right.

'Everyone ready and accounted for?' Colm's dad shouted.

It was tricky to bring seven kids to a football match, luckily Fitzgerald Stadium was just a ten-minute walk away! Colm's mam had packed ham sandwiches and crisps and Capri-Sun packets for everybody.

'Who's going to win the Munster final today?' Colm's dad asked as they started their walk.

'Kerry!' all of his siblings shouted in unison.

There was a phenomenal buzz in the town ahead of the final. Kerry had defeated Cork, the reigning All-Ireland champions, in the semi-final. After a few down years, there was hope that Kerry could be heading back to the glory days.

'Between 1975 and 1986, Kerry had won eight All-Irelands,' Colm's dad loved to remind his sons. 'No county had ever been that successful.'

Fitzgerald Stadium was packed to the gills. Colm had never heard so much noise before. Fans waved their flags during the parade. The stakes were so high. Lose this match and the Championship was over. There was no back-door system to save them.

All eyes were on Maurice Fitzgerald, Kerry's twenty-two-year-old forward. Maurice Fitz had made his debut for Kerry when he was just nineteen. He was seen as the future of Kerry football.

Colm sat beside his dad during the match. His happiest experiences were watching a football match beside his dad. They'd drive all around the county to watch Kerry club matches. It didn't matter if Dr Crokes were involved. Colm's dad just loved football, and Colm loved watching football with him. Colm would bring his Gaelic football with him to every match and kick points on the pitch when the teams went off for half-time.

From the opening throw-in, Colm could sense it would be an amazing Munster final. Limerick were underdogs. Both sets of supporters screamed at the top of their lungs. Limerick managed to score 3-12. It was not enough. Kerry had a bit more class. They scored 23 points and it was just enough to win. Maurice Fitz scored 12 points. At the full time whistle, Colm and his siblings all sprinted onto the pitch. Colm ran right for Maurice Fitz with magic marker.

'Can you sign my shirt, Maurice?' Colm asked.

'Sure thing,' he said.

Once they got home after the match, all of his siblings stayed in to have chips and watch the highlights of the match on *The Sunday Game*. But not Colm. He was too excited and headed to the Ardshan back green, on his own.

Colm stood in the middle of the green and imagined that he was part of the new generation.

He did the commentary himself, *'Thanks for tuning into Radio Kerry, we're live at a sold-out Croke Park where it is all level between Kerry and Dublin in the All-Ireland final ... There are three minutes of injury time to be played in the second half ... Kerry have the ball... in comes a high ball into to the Hill 16 end. Young Colm Cooper leaps for the ball. He catches! He turns! He shoots! He scores! Goal! Goal for Kerry! The boy from Ardshanavooly has put the Kingdom in front.'*

Colm jumped as high as he could and tried to punch the sky. He imagined the fans chanting his name. 'Coo-per! Coo-per! Coo-per!' They'd lift him on their shoulders and carry him all the way back to Killarney.

In that moment, he could feel it happening. It was more than just a daydream.

CHAPTER 4

DR CROKES IN THE ALL-IRELAND FINAL

'Colm,' his mother shouted. 'Come in for your dinner.'

Colm was out on the Ardshan green, practising his kicking. He raced in for his dinner and found his whole family at the table. It was exactly two weeks before the 1992 All-Ireland club final. Colm's club Dr Crokes were in the final against Thomas Davis from Dublin. Even better, his big brothers Danny and Mike were members of the Dr Crokes' squad. The game would take place on St Patrick's Day in Croke Park. Colm and his whole family would be there to roar on the Crokes.

'Two weeks from today,' Colm's mam said, as she passed a plate of potatoes around. 'What do you think about that?'

There was all kinds of excitement in the Cooper household. The previous autumn, they had won the Kerry title for the first time since 1914. There were wild celebrations in Killarney for days after.

Amazingly, Dr Crokes then won the Munster club title. They beat the champions of Limerick, Tipp and Cork. Then they flew to England to play a London club in the quarterfinal. Then they beat a Corofin from Galway in the semi-final.

No one could believe it.

It had been a few years since Kerry had played in Croke Park, so everyone in Killarney was thrilled by the idea of a trip to capital.

Colm was the most excited of anybody. He had been there for every kick along the way. He'd been there at every Dr Crokes training session. He'd collect loose footballs and set up cone drills. He wanted to be as close to the team as possible.

The match couldn't come quickly enough. It would be Colm's first trip to Croke Park. He had only seen Croke Park on *The Sunday Game* and on *Kerry's Golden Years*. It was amazing to think his brothers would be playing on that same famous pitch.

There was a knock on the front door. Teddy, the chairman of Dr Crokes, and John, the club secretary, were outside the house. It was strange that they were visiting the Coopers at home at night. Colm feared they had bad news about the All-Ireland.

'Well, lads,' Teddy the club secretary said to Danny and Mike. 'How are you feeling about the All-Ireland?'

'Great now,' Danny said. 'We're moving well in training.'

'Yerra, we'll give it a lash,' Mike said.

'I've no doubt you will,' John said.

'We're actually here to have a word with young Colm,' Teddy said.

Colm was startled. What could they possibly want with him?

'Colm, you've been everywhere with the team this season,' John said. 'We want to be sure you're at the match on St Patrick's Day.'

'Well, he was planning on travelling up with us,' Colm's mam said.

'That's great,' Teddy said. 'But Colm, we want you to be the official Dr Crokes mascot.'

Colm looked at his parents. He didn't really know what that meant.

'What would it involve? Could you explain it a bit more?' Colm's father asked.

'Ah, it's nothing too serious,' John said. 'You'd travel to Dublin with the team and be in the dugout during the match. You'd collect balls for the lads during warm-ups, just like you do now.'

'You're our good luck charm,' Danny said. 'We need you on the pitch.'

'What do you say?' Teddy said.

'Sure!' Colm said. He'd be going to the match anyway, so of course he loved the opportunity to be even closer to the action.

That night, and pretty much every night over the next two weeks, Colm could barely sleep. He had so many butterflies in his stomach. He'd lie in bed staring at his ceiling, thinking about Croke Park. He wondered if it was as big as it looked on TV. Once he even dreamed he was called in as a substitute during the match.

As the All-Ireland final grew nearer, all of Killarney became obsessed with the All-Ireland. It was all people talked about in school or at training. Danny and Mike had to take an afternoon out of work so they could be measured for blazers for the match. The club was treating it like the FA Cup final.

A week before the match, Danny came home from training with a plastic bag.

'Colm, this is for you for the All-Ireland,' Danny said. Inside the bag was a beautiful brand-new, kid-sized black and amber tracksuit with the Crokes crest on it. They wanted him to feel like he was an actual member of the team. Colm ran upstairs and put it on.

'Perfect fit,' his mam said.

He felt so proud. Even though he was only eight years old, he felt like a part of the team.

CHAPTER 5

AT CROKE PARK

The day before the All-Ireland club final, Colm, Danny and Mike piled into the family car and they drove to Killarney train station. Danny and Mike were wearing blazers with the Dr Crokes patch. Colm was wearing his Dr Crokes tracksuit.

The team would take the train to Heuston station and spend the night in a hotel in Malahide.

St Patrick's Day was on a Tuesday that year. Being the Dr Crokes' mascot meant Colm got to miss a day of school for the trip up to Dublin. Colm loved being the mascot!

'Can you believe that we're actually going to play in Croke Park?' Mike said, as they approached Killarney train station.

'Lads, playing in Croke Park is the greatest honour any GAA player will ever experience. Do your family proud tomorrow,' his father said.

Before boarding the train, the Dr Crokes coach Tatler O'Sullivan called everyone together.

'We can't leave Killarney without a team photo,' he said. The entire Dr Crokes team lined up in two rows. Colm wasn't sure where to stand.

'Gooch, you're in the middle,' Tatler shouted. He gave Colm the match football.

'On the count of three,' the photographer said, 'say "Up the Crokes!"'

'One...two...three....'

'Up the Crokes!!!' Colm roared in unison with everyone else.

Colm sat beside his brothers on train. A lot of Crokes fans had stayed on at the station to wave them off. Colm felt so many emotions as the train pulled out of Killarney. He was so excited to be a part of the team. He also was nervous and also a little bit scared to be travelling to Dublin without his parents. It was his very first time heading to Dublin.

'It's mad, isn't it, Colm? Croke Park,' Danny said

to him as the train pulled into Heuston station.

'It's crazy!' Colm said.

Even if he didn't have his parents, at least he had his two oldest brothers to look after him. Colm shared a hotel room with Mark and Danny. They all went to bed early that night so they'd be fully-rested for the big match.

They set an alarm for 7am and the team had a huge breakfast with eggs, rashers, sausages and toast. This meal would have to keep them going for the whole day. The team bus took them to Croke Park. Colm had never seen a stadium so big before. The bus drove down Jones's Road and towards a special entrance for teams and TV crews that went down under the stadium. A guard waved them into the stadium. It was *really* happening.

As the Crokes players changed out of the dressing rooms and into their kits, Colm gathered the bibs and water bottles.

'Head out to the pitch to loosen up!' Tatler O'Sullivan roared at the team.

They sprinted out onto the pitch and Colm followed them. As Colm neared the pitch, his path was blocked by a large man in a high-viz vest with a strong Dublin accent.

'Sorry, young man. You're not allowed on the pitch,' he said. 'From here on, it's grown-ups only. You'll have to turn back.'

Colm didn't know what to say. He was so close to the pitch, he could smell the freshly cut grass. He couldn't go back now, surely. Tears began to well up behind his eyes.

But before that could happen, Peter, the Dr Crokes goalie, walked over to the steward. He'd been the last out of the dressing room and heard the whole conversation.

'This lad is part of our team,' Peter said. He stood very close to the steward. 'And he's coming out with us.'

The steward didn't know what to say. He clearly didn't fancy an argument with Peter.

'Pardon me, son,' he said and allowed Colm to pass.

'Stay close to me, Gooch,' Peter said. 'In case we met any more stewards!'

Peter sprinted onto the pitch and Colm ran as fast to stick with him. What a feeling! His heart was beating so fast. He felt like the luckiest kid in the world.

The pitch was bigger than any pitch he'd ever seen. It was twenty times the size of the Dr Crokes pitch. Colm looked out into the stands, to see if he recognised any of his family. There were too many people, though!

For the warm up, Colm rolled out balls to the Crokes team as they took shots on goal. Colm took a sneaky shot at one stage and put it past Peter. He was delighted with the goal but Peter definitely was not impressed. He put another one in the top corner, just out of Peter's reach. Colm decided he wouldn't take any more shots on goal, and concentrated on collecting balls.

Tatler called everyone into a circle for a final team talk.

'Lads, most of you have never played here at Croke Park. We may never get a chance to play here again. This is our chance. We're bringing that cup back to Killarney.'

Tatler spoke with such confidence that Colm knew they were going to win.

Colm watched the match from the Hogan Stand dugout, beside the subs and physios. It was tit-for-tat in the opening stages of the game. Thomas Davis were a savage team. But then Pat O'Shea, their best player, put Dr Crokes ahead with a goal in the 13th minute. Colm jumped for joy.

Dinny, one of the subs, lifted him off the ground.

'This is our day, Gooch,' he said.

Dr Crokes had a narrow lead going into half-time.

A few minutes into the second half, Danny was involved in an incident with a Thomas Davis player. Colm hadn't seen the incident, but Danny looked very worried. Colm could hear a few of the Thomas Davis supporters calling in their Dublin accents for the ref to take action. The ref had a word with Danny before reaching into his pocket. Red card. Danny tried to plead with him but it made no difference. He walked to the bench with his head in his hands.

'C'mon fellas, you'll need to dig deeper now,' Tatler shouted.

Thomas Davis came at them with everything they had. Still Dr Crokes clung on to their one-point lead. It was so nerve-wracking. Colm didn't think they'd hold on.

Then came the final whistle. *Peep. Peep. Peep.* Dr

Crokes were All-Ireland champions! The final score was Dr Crokes 1-11 Thomas Davis 0-13.

Colm ran onto the pitch with everyone from the dugout. He sprinted for his brothers. Everyone from Killarney followed from the stands. There were hundreds of people on the pitch, shouting and roaring. Colm knew almost all of them to see. It was crazy to see them all here in Dublin. Then his mam and dad found him.

His dad picked him up off the ground.

'Well done, Colm!' his mam said.

'They couldn't have done it without you,' his dad said.

His sisters and brothers were with them and the whole family formed a big circle and hugged.

Then the time came to lift the Cup.

Seanie, the Dr Crokes captain, was given the microphone to make a speech.

'It could have been anybody's game but the gods were with us today,' he said into the microphone before wishing 'three cheers' to the Thomas Davis team.

Before Colm left the pitch, he said to himself, 'I'll be back here some day.'

Lots of Crokes fans celebrated in Heuston station while they waited for the train back to Killarney. Colm had so many packets of Taytos he thought he might burst. The Dr Crokes players poured champagne into the Andy Merrigan Cup and drank from it. Being All-Ireland champions was a tremendous feeling.

The Dr Crokes team photo was on the front page of *The Kerryman* that Wednesday. Colm was front and centre in that photo, holding the match ball. The headlines read 'All-Ireland glory for Dr Crokes' and 'Just like the great Kerry days from 70s and 80s'.

There was pandemonium in Killarney for weeks afterwards. When the Dr Crokes team visited The Mercy with the Merrigan Cup, Colm got to leave class for the day and tour the school with the cup.

Colm felt like a celebrity walking around into fifth class and sixth class with the Dr Crokes captain. More than anything, he hoped he'd get a chance to play in Croke Park again someday.

CHAPTER 6

COLM GETS AN EDUCATION IN KERRY FOOTBALL

'Colm! It's a minute to ten,' his dad shouted. 'You're going to miss your bus to training.'

Colm was upstairs brushing his teeth. He hurriedly spat out the toothpaste, grabbed his gear bag from his bedroom and sprinted down the stairs. Colm was ten-years-old and training with the Dr Crokes U12 team today.

'Bye, Mam!' Colm shouted as he ran out the door. He didn't even have time to kiss his mam goodbye.

Most of the Ardshan kids were waiting along the wall of the estate. The Horan brothers were there, as was Tommy O'Regan. Tommy's grandfather had won the four-in-a-row with Kerry back in the 1930s, Colm's dad had told him once. Kerry GAA was very strong in their estate.

Like clockwork, Mr Buckley's bus arrived on the dot of ten. Every Saturday he'd collect the kids from all the nearby estates and bring them to the Crokes clubhouse on Lewis Road to train. After training, Mr Buckley would take all the kids home.

The grown-ups around Dr Crokes gave so much of their free time and energy to the club, and asked for so little back in return.

'You'll pay me back by winning Kerry titles, won't you, lads?' Mr Buckley joked once when asked about all the driving he'd do.

All the kids on the bus were wearing their black and amber Dr Crokes kit. Colm was obsessed with the club, he knew everything about it. Their crest featured a football, two hurleys, a bishop's mitre, two jumping stags and the words '*Cul Dirne*', which meant 'Tell us'.

Colm knew if he was ever going to play for the Dr Crokes senior team, he'd have to do a lot of work on his own.

He'd learned from the football matches with his older brothers that he needed to be skilful with both feet to compete with the bigger lads.

There was a place off the Ardshan green where Colm liked to go to practise kicking. There was a metal bar stuck into the ground and it was perfect for target practice. Colm would start with his stronger foot – the left foot – and practise kicking the ball from the ground. He'd hit the target fifty times then switch to his right boot. He'd hit the target fifty more times.

Then he'd practise kicking the ball from hand, starting with the left foot, and then switching to the right again: fifty shots per boot.

He'd stay out there taking target practice until he heard his Mam's voice.

'Colm, it's time for bed!' she would shout.

Just ten more kicks, he'd tell himself.

'Colm, it's after 10pm!' she'd shout a few minutes later.

Just five more kicks, he'd tell himself.

'Colm, I'm not going to call you again!!'

'Okay, okay, I'm coming,' he'd shout and race in.

He'd sleep with his football beside his bed so it

would be the first thing he'd touch when he got up in the morning.

So much of his life centred around the club. Coach Pádraig was leading today's training session. He was Colm's favourite coach.

'Lads, today we're going to head to Fitzgerald Stadium so you can get a sense of what it's like to play for Kerry.'

Fitzgerald Stadium was just a short walk away. The stadium had hosted so many famous Munster finals over the years. It was a clear afternoon and the majestic McGillycuddy Reeks were visible in the distance. Colm thought this must be the most beautiful place on earth. He stepped onto the pitch and felt goosebumps from all the history.

Coach Pádraig ran them through a few drills before calling all the lads in.

'Huddle together, lads,' Coach Pádraig shouted. He liked nothing more than talking about Gaelic football.

'Great training today, lads,' Coach Pádraig said. 'Isn't it a brilliant thing to be out here at Fitzgerald Stadium, kicking a football around, with the sun shining down us? I'd call it freedom.'

The lads laughed. They knew they were in for a lecture.

'You're all kicking the ball wonderfully today lads, great to see it.' He paused for a moment. 'Fellas, I have a question for you. What's the most important part of the Gaelic footballer's body?'

'Uh, the foot?' Tommy O'Regan said. 'That's why they call it football.'

The lads laughed.

'Integral yes, but I said *most* important,' Coach Pádraig said.

'The shoulder?' Billy McCarthy said.

'Spoken like a true cornerback, Billy!' Coach Pádraig said. 'No, no, it's right here.'

Coach Pádraig pointed to his brain.

'Yes, you need a boot to kick points. And you need hands and shoulders to mark your opposition. But without a sharp brain, you'll never make it as a Kerry footballer.'

Everyone was listening closely now.

'Boys, we're from Kerry. We're the aristocrats of Gaelic football,' he said.

Everyone laughed again. 'Aristocrats' was a funny word to describe Gaelic footballers, but Colm understood exactly what he meant. He was talking about playing with class.

'Now up in Dublin, they'd scoff at you for saying that, but it's true and why hide from it? But lads there's a responsibility that comes with that. It's not enough to simply win matches. It's how you play the game. We have a duty to play beautifully.'

He said the word beautifully with five syllables: *bee-you-tiff-oooooo-leeeee*.

'In Brazil, they have soccer. In New Zealand, they have rugby. In Kerry, lads, we have Gaelic football, it's what Kerry people were born to do.'

'The beautiful thing is each and every one of you can wear that green and gold shirt if you earn it. But if you want to play for Kerry, you'll need to train your brain as well as your body. You'll need to see the pitch in its entirety. You'll need to anticipate passes five seconds before your marker. You'll need to attempt passes that the opposition wouldn't think of in a hundred years.'

'That's what made those Kerry legends so special. They played the game smarter than anyone had ever played it before.'

'Gaelic football can be a hard man's game, too. And

every now and again, we'll need to get tough. But when we can, we play our way. The Kerry way, the beautiful way.

Coach Pádraig paused and let his words sink in. Some of the lads looked bored, but Colm understood completely. From playing in Ardshan, he'd learned to see the whole match unfold seconds before most of the other kids. If only his body would catch up!

'Now who's up for a game of forwards-and-backs?' Coach Pádraig yelled. The lads all roared in agreement.

CHAPTER 7

GAME AGAINST KILCUMMIN U14

I t was a beautiful Saturday afternoon in Kerry, but Colm was nervous. He often felt nervous before matches, but he was very nervous today. The Dr Crokes U14s had been having a terrible season. Today they had a huge match against Kilcummin, a club just outside Killarney.

The whole county was swept up in Gaelic football fever. In just a few weeks, Kerry were due to contest their first All-Ireland final in 11 years. That week, RTÉ had sent a reporter to Killarney to interview young GAA players about this Kerry team.

They filmed a Dr Crokes training session and their reporter Marty Morrissey interviewed Colm about his own football connections.

'I have four brothers in the Dr Crokes senior team, so I have a lot to live up to, really,' Colm said.

His parents all laughed when they heard him say it on the telly a few nights later, but it was true. That autumn, Colm had started secondary school in The Sem, which was traditionally the best colleges' Gaelic football team in Kerry. The Sem had won many Hogan Cups over the years. The legendary Kerry footballer and current manager Páidí Ó Sé was a past pupil. Colm played with The Sem team but he'd struggled to make an impact with them. Fionn, Gavin and Pat, three of his teammates from The Sem, also played for Kilcummin. Colm had to prove he was as good as they were.

Colm's dad drove him to the match. Colm loved travelling to games with his dad – well he liked the journeys to matches at least! Colm was usually too angry to talk after a Dr Crokes defeat, and there'd been a lot of those lately.

'Where will Pat The Bag play you today, Colm?' his dad asked. (One of the great things about Kerry GAA was the nicknames: from Eoin Bomber Liston to Pat The Bag O'Sullivan, everyone seemed to have a memorable nickname.)

'I think it will be midfield again,' Colm said sadly. Colm knew his best position was in the forward line. But his coach Pat The Bag O'Sullivan played him in midfield because he could have a greater influence on the game. In the midfield, he could clean up the dirty ball from the kickout and get the Dr Crokes attack moving. His skills as a forward were wasted since there was no one to pass to him.

'It's important to know how to play every position on the pitch,' Colm's dad said. 'This experience will make you a better footballer.'

'I know, Dad,' Colm said. 'You're right.'

Colm had been having a brilliant season with Dr Crokes. He was getting a bit taller. His kicking was improving. He could put spin on the ball now, and make the football arc like a banana in the sky. The games at Ardshan had made him tough as well: a few defenders had learned the hard way that he was not some bean pole that would tumble to the ground with the slightest touch.

But Colm couldn't change the performance of the other fourteen players on his team. To be blunt about it, the Dr Crokes U14s were a shambles. They simply weren't at the level of the best clubs in Kerry, and it drove Colm crazy.

Colm hated losing more than anything. Some of the lads on the team didn't seem to mind it, but losing made Colm sick. Colm couldn't do everything, much as he tried.

'Let me ask you a question,' his dad said. 'Which do you enjoy more? Playing Gaelic with Dr Crokes or playing soccer with Killarney Celtic?'

'Hmmm.' Colm said. He thought about it, and he didn't know the answer.

Colm loved playing football with Killarney Celtic. The team was good and Colm played up front as the main striker. He loved banging in goals. Deep down, Colm dreamed of being the first Kerryman to play for Liverpool.

But Dr Crokes was his club. Even though he was only fourteen, he still felt a kind of responsibility to it.

'I love them both, Dad,' Colm said.

'And it's a good thing you don't have to choose,' Colm's dad said. 'When I was your age, you couldn't play GAA and football. The GAA wouldn't allow it. We've come a long way.'

'Maybe I'll be the first Kerryman to play at Croke

Park and Anfield,' Colm replied.

They both laughed.

'If you can dream it, you can do it,' Colm's dad said.

Talking to his dad helped Colm take his mind off the game. Sometimes his mam told him he took sports too seriously.

'It's not life and death,' Colm's mam said a few weeks ago, after Colm came home in a strop after a defeat. 'It's only football.'

Colm didn't agree. It felt like the most important thing in the whole world.

Pat The Bag pulled Colm aside in the middle of the warm-ups.

'Colm, we're going to start you in midfield again today,' said Coach Pat. 'We need you to be like the conductor in an orchestra. Set the tempo with your passes.'

'Sure thing,' Colm said.

As the two teams took their positions for the throw-in, Colm noticed the Kilcummin defenders were all taller than the Dr Crokes players. He'd have to be crafty if he was going to get the ball into them.

'Tap it backwards off the throw-in,' Colm whispered to Seanie, his partner in midfield. 'I'll be ready.'

When the ref threw the ball in, Seanie did exactly as planned. He won the ball and tapped it right into Colm's hands. Colm charged ahead. He saw that Big Mike, their full forward had a step on his marker and Colm fired a laser of a pass towards him. It bounced once off the ground and landed perfectly in Big Mike's chest.

Unfortunately Big Mike dropped the pass and the ball was cleared out by the Kilcummin defence.

A few minutes later, Colm pounced on a breaking ball after a Dr Crokes kickout. He soloed past one defender, and then shimmied by another. Paudie, the Crokes right corner forward was making a run at goal and Colm spotted it. Colm fired a pass perfectly into the empty space between the last Kilcummin defender and their goalie. It was the perfect place for Paudie to receive the pass.

Only Paudie had stopped his run. The ball bounced harmlessly into the hands of the goalie.

Colm threw his hands up to the skies and shouted.

When two Kilcummin players collided off the ball, Pat The Bag ran on the field with a water bottle for Colm even though he wasn't very thirsty.

'Have a drink of this and listen to me a second Colm,' Pat The Bag said. 'Now I know it's frustrating that the rest of the lads aren't at your level. But we live as a team and we die as a team.'

'I know, Coach Pat.'

'I need you to remember one thing. These aren't just your teammates. They're your clubmates. They're your brothers. You all represent the same community. You're their captain. Captains lead. Don't forget that.'

Colm looked up at his teammates. They were freckly, fair-haired kids like the Kilcummin players, but he grew up with these lads.

After the restart, Colm took a high ball and beat his man.

He was looking for options in the forward line when he heard Seanie's voice in is ear.

'Feed it to me, Gooch,' Seanie said as he sprinted forward, up the right flank.

Colm fisted the ball into open space and let Seanie run onto it. Seanie caught the ball and kicked the ball from the 45 metre line. Amazingly it cleared the post! Everyone on the Dr Crokes sideline cheered!

Colm had only seen grown-ups kick points from that distance.

Seanie pumped his fist like he won the All-Ireland. Colm had forgotten what it was like to enjoy himself while playing Gaelic football. Dr Crokes lost the match by seven points but at full time, all of the Crokes players mobbed Seanie.

'Another tough defeat,' Colm's dad said when Colm got in the car

'Yeah but wasn't Seanie's point amazing?' Colm said.

'Aye, it sure was,' his dad said.

CHAPTER 8

IN THE KERRY DEVELOPMENT SQUAD

Colm was on a bus to Cork with some of the most talented young footballers in Kerry. A few weeks before his fifteenth birthday, Colm was invited into the Kerry U16 development squad.

The team were travelling to Páirc Uí Chaoimh, for a challenge match against the Cork U16s. After this match, the squad would break up for a few months. The best players would be invited into the Kerry minor panel for next season.

The other lads on the bus came from all over Kerry. They shared the same goal: they dreamed of playing for their county some day. Colm was first and foremost a Dr Crokes player, and he would always be one. But all young players dreamed of making the breakthrough to the county team. Intercounty football got serious at minor level, which was U18 at the time. Players who were good enough would train with two teams: their club *and* their county team.

He trained one night a week with the development squad, alongside his training with the Dr Crokes team.

The stakes were very high with this development squad, and all the lads knew it. This was the easiest way to make it onto the Kerry minor panel. Break into the Kerry minor team, and then you might get called into the Kerry U21s. Make your mark with the Kerry U21s and then you might get called into the Kerry senior panel. Make your mark with the Kerry senior panel and you might just become a Kerry legend.

'It's like a train journey,' was how his dad described it. 'You go from station to station to station. But it helps to be on from the beginning!'

His brothers were all decent club footballers – Mark and Danny were club All-Ireland winners after all – but even during their best seasons with Dr Crokes, they were never considered good enough to play for the Kingdom.

'County football is a different class,' Colm's dad said once. 'The best of the best.'

Colm had put everything into his weekly training sessions with the Kerry U16s. But training with them was a bittersweet experience. On one hand, he felt so lucky to be surrounded by such talented players from all across the county. There were lads from Tralee, and Kenmare, and Rathmore, and Tarbert. It was so much different from playing with his club, where he was the best player by a country mile.

But Colm had struggled to make an impression on the management team. In the first training match, he'd come up against a six-foot-tall defender with farmer strength from Valentia Island named Manus. Colm had never been marked by a defender like Manus before. Colm tried to beat him down the wing but Manus simply stuck his shoulder out and knocked him over.

It was like running into a tree.

Manus picked him right up off the ground.

'Didn't mean to hurt you there,' Manus said. 'We play a bit rougher out on Valentia!'

Ever since that first training session, Colm had struggled to get a game.

After one of the training sessions, he overheard two of the selectors discussing some of the players.

'He's got decent touch, sure, but is he too skinny?' one said.

No name had been mentioned, but Colm knew the selectors had been talking about him. Colm tried not to get angry about it. The forwards on the team were all very good, but Colm knew he could hold his own. He just needed a chance.

Colm had never been more nervous for a match. He knew this was his last chance to make an impression on the team management.

On the bus to Cork, Colm sat next to a lad from the village of Dromid in south Kerry named Declan O'Sullivan.

Declan was an incredible footballer. More importantly he was a very sound lad. He went to Coláiste na Sceilge in Cahirsiveen. They'd played against the Sem a few times. Colm had never seen a footballer as good as Declan. He had pace to burn and amazing vision. He seemed destined to be a star for Kerry.

'If you're on the pitch today, I'll look for you,' Declan said. 'Just be patient and your chance will come.'

'I will, thanks Dec,' Colm said.

Colm looked around the bus. He'd never been surrounded by so many good footballers.

These were the players who would be wearing the Kerry jersey and hopefully lifting the Sam Maguire in Croke Park in ten years' time.

The bus pulled into the Páirc Uí Chaoimh car park. Paul their manager stood up.

'Listen close,' he said. 'Here's the fifteen lads who'll be starting today.'

Colm prayed he'd hear his name amongst the forwards.

He didn't hear his name.

'If you haven't heard your name, you're in with the subs.'

Declan could tell how disappointed Colm was.

'We'll need an impact sub against these Cork lads, they're fierce,' he told Colm.

'I'll be ready,' Colm replied.

Colm found it hard to watch the match from the sideline. Cork weren't great but the lads in the full forward line were putting easy shots at goal wide.

Colm felt like walking right up to Paul and saying 'If you put me in, I'll convert those. You can trust me.'

But it didn't work that way. You had to be given a chance.

Colm vigorously loosened up along the sideline, with the hope Paul might have forgot him. But with five minutes left in the game, Colm began to accept reality. He wasn't going to get on. Paul wanted to win the match with the fifteen players on the pitch. Colm took a seat on the bench. It was the loneliest place in the world.

The Kerry U16s beat Cork by two points but it didn't really matter to Colm. He congratulated the lads but it was half-hearted. He didn't speak to anyone on the ninety-minute drive back to Cork.

When they arrived in Kerry, Paul gathered the entire development squad into a huddle.

'We've grown a lot over the past few months, lads,' he said. 'We've got the bones of a solid minor team here. The selectors from the minor team will be in touch with some of you. For the others, we appreciate your effort. Either way, the future of Kerry football is in a good place.'

As Colm was waiting for his dad to collect him, Paul approached him.

'Thanks for your time these last few months, Colm,' Paul said. 'You've got a lot of potential. Best of luck with your club.'

Paul didn't mention anything about training with the minors. Colm could read between the lines.

'How did you play?' Colm's dad asked when Colm sat in the car.

'I didn't get on,' Colm said. 'I didn't play a second.'

Colm was too angry to talk to his dad on the ride home. When they pulled into the estate, Colm's dad stopped the car and looked at him.

'You know, Colm, there's more to football than Kerry. You were part of a club before this development squad. And you'll be part of a club after.'

Colm was too hurt to admit it, but he knew his dad was right.

Back in the house, Colm didn't feel like talking to anyone. He ran right upstairs and closed his door. He felt like crying. But before he could he saw the photo of the 1992 All-Ireland-winning Dr Crokes. There were his brothers. And there he was, right in the middle of it all.

He thought of the players on his Dr Crokes team, lads he'd been playing football with since he was six years old.

Through thick and through thin, he was part of a club, and no one could ever take that away. Even if he never wore the Kerry jersey, he'd have his club. That was something special.

CHAPTER 9

WELCOME TO THE DR CROKES SENIOR TEAM

I t was a frigid winter night in January, in the first days after the start of the new millennium. Colm was seventeen years old. He could feel the cold in his bones. His breath looked like white smoke when he exhaled.

It was the first night of training for the Dr Crokes senior team for the 2000 season. Before Christmas, Colm had received a phone call from Donal, one of Coach Harry's selectors.

'Colm, you were training a bit with us last summer,' Donal said. 'We think you're ready to play a big part of the panel this season. We want you on the panel, and training with us every night.'

Colm was delighted. Even if he didn't start any matches, he knew he'd learn so much training with the senior team.

Coach Harry welcomed them all. Harry's selectors Donal and Paudie stood behind him. They were his assistants who helped him with the coaching.

'If you look around,' Coach Harry said. 'You'll see that there's no footballs here. Winter training is all about building the fitness that will get us to September and October. Tonight we're going to be working off those Christmas dinners!'

All of the older lads in the panel groaned.

'Let's start with twenty-five laps of the pitch,' Donal shouted. 'No cutting corners!'

Roland, their captain, led the thirty-man panel on their way. Colm didn't mind the running, though he much preferred playing matches. He stayed to the back of the group during the jogging.

'I don't know if I'll make it to February, lads,' said Connie, one of the oldest members of the team.

There was a lot of experience and a lot of youth in the Dr Crokes senior squad, but not much in between. There were some older lads in their thirties who had carried the club for years. These guys had kids of their own. They'd given everything to Dr Crokes. A few had even played for Kerry.

These men had been Colm's heroes when he was the Dr Crokes mascot. Now they were his team-mates.

There also were a lot of players who were Colm's age. As Colm jogged, he counted eight lads who were U21. He and Eanna Kavanagh, a defender, were still in secondary school in the Sem.

All four of Colm's brothers were there as well.

In one way or another, his whole life seemed to be represented in this group of footballers jogging round and round a football pitch on this freezing January night.

All last season, Dr Crokes had struggled to get the numbers to training. The team had been pretty poor for a few years now and people weren't willing to make the commitment. Colm knew this was a massive chance to make an impression.

'Lads, let's begin the season with some honesty,' Coach Harry said, after the laps had been completed. 'No one in Kerry fancies us this year. If we're to achieve anything, it's going to come from you lot.

'If you work hard enough and train hard enough, you can start in my team. I don't care how old you are.'

'If we're going to get anywhere, the old lads and the younger lads are going to have to work together.'

Roland called the whole squad into a huddle.

'One word, lads,' Roland said. 'Belief. We need to believe we are the best team in Kerry. Before we can do that, we need to believe in each other.'

Colm linked shoulders with players twice his age. He felt part of something bigger.

CHAPTER 10

COLM GETS HIS CHANCE

Later that year, Colm got a call from the Kerry county board. He was wanted for a trial match between the Kerry minor team and the Kerry junior team, which was made up of older players who were almost good enough to play with the senior intercounty team. Even though Colm wasn't officially part of the minor panel, he'd been asked to participate.

'Will you give it a lash?' his father asked.

Colm was still stung by being overlooked for minor panel the previous year, but training with the Dr Crokes senior team had been a brilliant experience.

'I suppose I have nothing to lose,' Colm said.

Play well in this game and he knew might be called into the minor panel.

Colm had been training with the Dr Crokes senior team two nights a week. His game had come on leaps and bounds in just a few months. If he was good enough for the Dr Crokes senior team, surely, Colm thought, he was good enough for the Kerry minors.

There was very little chit-chat between him and his dad on the drive to Tralee for the match.

'The county board must have gotten wind of how well you're doing the Crokes team.'

'Maybe,' Colm replied. 'I don't want to sit on the bench again. I want to play.'

When he arrived in the dressing room, Colm found a team sheet taped to the wall. Colm was not in the starting 15. His heart sank a bit.

'Typical,' he thought. But he snapped himself out of negative thinking. 'My performance will be even more impressive coming from a sub,' he said to himself.

Colm watched a lot of the match from the side-lines, and tried to stay loose and ready. The minor team were made up of players from the previous year's development squad. There were some decent players, like Declan O'Sullivan. A few selectors from the minor team and county board sat in the stands with clipboards. These were the people to impress. After about twenty minutes, the corner forward on the minor team took a heavy knock going for a 50–50 ball.

'Cooper, you're on,' one of selectors roared. 'Let's see what you can do.'

Colm sprinted onto the field like an angry bull. He'd be waiting for this moment and he was going to seize it.

His marker from the junior team was a big lad, but Colm had studied the match closely and knew he lacked agility. As soon as the minor team had possession, Colm flashed for a ball. Declan sent in a perfect pass. Colm dinked left and then shot off his bad foot from about twenty-five yards out. Point.

Colm pumped his fist.

'Good man,' Colm's dad shouted from the side-line.

Minutes later, the minors attacked again. Their full forward rocketed a shot in at goal. The keeper parried it away but the ball landed right in front of Colm. He struck the rebound sweetly into the bottom right corner of the net.

'You need a bit of luck as well,' Colm thought.

The Kerry juniors tried marking Colm with a different defender, but it didn't make a massive difference. When the ref blew the final whistle, Colm had scored 1-4.

All the forwards from the minor team congratulated him after the match.

'Well done, Colm,' Declan said. 'You'll be back with us after that.'

It felt great to be accepted by the minor team, but Colm knew that he belonged with these guys.

'Well played tonight, Cooper,' Charlie Nelligan, the Kerry minor manager and himself a Kerry legend said to Colm said in the dressing room. There was no talk of another trial with the minor panel, however, just a handshake.

'They have to bring you back after that tonight,' Colm's dad said on the drive back to Killarney. 'You were sensational.'

'We'll see,' Colm said. 'Either way, they'll remember my name tonight.'

The next night, the phone rang as the Coopers

ate their dinner. Colm's dad answered.

'Hello, Charlie,' Colm's dad said. It was the Kerry minor manager calling. It sounded like a serious phone call. Colm's father didn't get many words in.

After he hung up, Colm's dad looked sad.

'I've some news for you, Colm,' his dad said.

Oh, not again, Colm thought.

His father's face lit up all of a sudden.

'That was Charlie Nelligan. They want you to join the minor panel. And they want you to start at corner forward for them.'

Colm jumped out of his seat and hugged his dad.

Finally, Colm thought. Finally.

CHAPTER II

BROTHERS IN ARMS

A month later, the Dr Crokes senior team bus departed Killarney for the quarterfinal of the 2000 Kerry club Championship. They had been drawn away against one of the county's best teams, South Kerry. The match would take place in Waterville on the edge of the Atlantic Ocean. Rain bucketed down and the wind howled. The weather was diabolical. The day was more suited to water polo than Gaelic football.

'These are the conditions the South Kerry boys will absolutely relish,' Coach Harry said as the bus passed through Killorglin.

Waterville could be a two-hour drive from Killarney if you met cattle on the road, or worse, slow-driving Americans. There were mountains to the left and there was ocean to the right. Colm had never been a part of anything like this in his career. This was Championship. It was another level. Everyone was very serious. It was like they were going to war.

At Tuesday in training, Coach Harry had called him and Eanna aside.

'Lads, we have a big match on Sunday. Our whole season depends on it,' he said. 'You're both going to start. Colm we need you to get at their defenders.'

Colm was shocked. Playing for the Dr Crokes senior team had always been his goal. He just didn't expect he'd be starting Championship matches by the time he was seventeen!

'Are you up for it, son?'

'Absolutely, Harry,' Colm said.

Colm was really nervous, but it was comforting to know how much family support he had. His parents and sisters would be in the stands, and his four brothers would be beside him on the pitch. All five Cooper brothers were named in the Dr Crokes starting fifteen. They all sat near each other on the bus.

'Mad, isn't it,' Vince said. 'A third of the Crokes

team are Coopers!'

'It must be a record, five brothers in one team,' Mike said.

'Colm, don't worry if any of those South Kerry lads start picking on you,' Danny said. 'There'll be four Coopers out there ready to look after you.'

'It'll be like being back in Ardshan,' Mark said.

Colm nodded. It would be such a tough game. South Kerry had a few players in the Kerry team that had won Munster that year, most notably Maurice Fitzgerald. It was the same Maurice Fitz who'd autographed Colm's jersey after the 1991 Munster final. Nine years later, Maurice Fitz was a three-time All-Star, an All-Ireland winner and a former Footballer of the Year. Colm had to pinch himself. He was sharing the pitch with one of the greatest Kerry forwards of them all.

When the bus pulled into the Waterville GAA ground, Coach Harry addressed the entire team.

'Lads, South Kerry have had an edge on us for years. But that changes today. We've got All-Ireland winners on this bus. We've got players like young Gooch here in front of me who can inspire a new generation. You lads have a Kerry title in you, I know it. The journey starts here.'

All the team roared.

'Now, we can't play pretty football in these conditions,' Harry said. 'We'll have to win ugly.'

After the warm ups, Colm took his place at corner forward. Beside him in the forward line were Pat O'Shea and Connie Murphy. They were twice as old as Colm. Both had played intercounty for Kerry.

Pat called the forward line together.

'Don't tell yourself you don't belong at this level,' Connie said to Colm. 'You do belong.'

Colm nodded.

'We've got the experience,' Pat said, with a wink. 'We just need you to supply the youth.'

Colm walked over to his marker.

'Welcome to Waterville,' the South Kerry corner-back said, and placed his hand out to be shaken.

'Thanks,' Colm said.

As soon as the referee blew the whistle and threw the ball in, Colm immediately found himself face down on the boggy turf. His marker had pushed him right over. He hadn't seen it coming. Colm hopped right up, as if he hadn't felt a thing.

Mark and Vince were already confronting Colm's marker.

'None of your dirty tricks,' Vince said, with two fistfuls of the South Kerry man's jersey in his hands.

It was a dire match in woeful conditions. Colm tried to give as much as he got from his marker. There weren't many chances to play free-flowing football. Halfway through the second half, Noel O'Leary of Dr Crokes attempted an ambitious, towering shot from distance.

He'd mangled the shot though, and it was falling short of the goal. With everyone around him ball watching, Colm found himself moving towards the ball. It was tumbling slowly out of the sky, and Colm jumped towards it. He leaped head-first through a traffic jam of bodies and blasted the ball with his fist. It rocketed into the back of the net.

Goal for Dr Crokes!

After a delay of a second or two, there was a huge roar from the travelling support from Killarney.

Colm dusted himself off – he was just grateful he didn't get a kick in the head after hurling his body at the ball. The goal was a nice bonus.

'Who taught you that, Cooper?' Pat asked with

an amazed look in his eye.

Colm just shrugged his shoulders, and tried to keep his head down. His defender wouldn't be pleased. Dr Crokes were ahead now. The goal gave them all the momentum they needed. When the ref blew for full time, the scoreboard said Dr Crokes 1-4 South Kerry 0-6. Colm's goal was the difference.

After the match, Maurice Fitzgerald walked right up to him to congratulate him.

'Well played,' he said. 'That was a great goal.'

'Thanks,' Colm said. Colm wasn't sure whether to call him Maurice or Maurice Fitz or Maurice Fitzgerald, so he just grinned awkwardly.

Then his parents and sisters swarmed around him.

'Colm, that was an amazing goal,' his mam said.

'Where'd that come from?' Geraldine asked.

'Practise on the Ardshan green, I guess,' Colm said.

A photographer from *The Kerryman* newspaper arranged all the Cooper brothers in a row for a photograph, aged youngest to oldest.

Colm hugged his dad after the photographer did his work. He'd never seen his dad so proud in his life.

'I'm the luckiest man alive today,' Colm's dad said. 'I've seen all of my sons win a Kerry championship match together.'

'We might be lifting the cup yet!' Mark said.

Colm couldn't have asked for anything more from his Dr Crokes Championship debut.

CHAPTER 12

A FIRST SHOT AT SILVERWARE

After beating South Kerry that wet day in Waterville, Dr Crokes had to play West Kerry in the semi-final. The Crokes were massive underdogs again but they managed to win on another soggy Kerry day.

It meant that as Colm began his final year in secondary school, he had two big events on his mind: the Leaving Cert and the Kerry County Final. Most of Colm's classmates at the Sem were worrying about the Leaving Cert, which they would be taking at the end of the school year.

Dr Crokes were up against An Ghaeltacht, from out in the Dingle Peninsula, in the county final. Colm got shivers the day he found out the opposition. There were so many famous players on that An Ghaeltacht team. There was the Ó Sé brothers, Páidí's nephews: Darragh and Tomás had already broken through with the Kerry team and young Marc won a minor All-Ireland with Kerry. There was Dara Ó Cinnéide and Aodhán Mac Gearailt. Colm had watched them win the All-Ireland with Kerry just two months ago. Now he was playing against them.

'No matter what happens, you'll get the taste of playing in a Kerry final,' Colm's dad. 'That's something valuable.'

Colm agreed, but he feared they might receive a hiding.

'The bookies have us as massive underdogs,' Eanna said to him at lunch one day. 'Eight to one, apparently! My dad says they're giving us no chance.'

'Imagine if we do it though,' Colm said. 'We'll be heroes.'

The final was at Austin Stack Park in Tralee. Harry announced the starting team on the Tuesday before the match. Colm would be starting in the full forward line.

'Just treat it like any other match,' Colm's dad had

told him a few weeks before the game. It was difficult to do that, because no one in the town treated it like any other match! A photographer visited the club a week before the match to take portraits of every player, and a photo of the entire squad. Then a tailor called in to measure them all for blazers. It was all a bit stressful.

'This must be like what the players in the Premiership have to deal with every week,' Colm thought.

A few days before the game, black and amber bunting went up around Ardshanavooly and all the nearby estates in Killarney.

People kept approaching Colm and wishing him good luck in the game. It happened in the shops, on the street, even in school. Some of the people he knew, others were strangers. For the first time in his life, Colm was experiencing something all elite sportspeople were very familiar with: pressure.

Colm and all his brothers decided to get haircuts on the day before the big match.

'It'll give us something to do other than thinking of the game,' Danny said.

Colm knew his team would need him to have a good game if they were to have any chance of winning the Kerry title. Having all of his brothers around made him less nervous.

When the Dr Crokes bus pulled into Tralee the next day, Colm and his teammates looked sharp and were ready for business.

After they togged out and warmed up, the Dr Crokes team gathered in the dressing room for the final preparations. The entire squad pulled into a circle. Connie stood into the middle of the group and addressed everyone.

'Lads, in that other dressing room, there's a bunch of lads who think that their name is already on that cup,' he said. 'It's taken us an awful long time to get back here. We've given so much for each other these last few months. For all the young lads in the room, I know this is only the start of your career.'

Connie looked right at Colm.

'But the likes of myself and some of the older lads here, this is our last chance. I'm thirty-five. It might sound selfish, but win it for us. We'll be sitting on those terraces for rest of our lives. Let's win today.'

Colm suddenly understood why the stakes were so high. He knew he couldn't let his clubmates down. They burst out of the dressing room, screaming and hollering. Colm wondered if any team in Ireland could stop them.

CHAPTER 13

'YOU'RE GOING TO HAVE TO DIG DEEP'

Austin Stack Park was packed with Gaelic fans hoping for a memorable game. It was another wild Kerry day. The coin toss meant that Crokes had the wind at their backs in the first half. The pressure would be on Colm and the other forwards to build up a score while they had the advantage.

During the parade, Colm could feel his muscles tensing up. He knew all of the greats of Kerry football were in the stand. Colm didn't want to think selfishly, but he knew there was no better showcase for his talents than a county final.

'We need ye to rack up a big score early, lads,' Harry shouted from the sideline towards the forwards. 'While we have the wind.'

The Crokes brought an intensity from the off. The backs flew into challenges, bursting in with shoulders, and then worked the ball up the pitch with quick hand passes. In the second minute, Colm broke free of his marker and shot from the edge of the D. The umpire waved the white flag. First score to Dr Crokes.

It was clear from the early exchanges that the An Ghaeltacht lads were not expecting the intensity that the Dr Crokes had brought to the game. The Crokes scored the first three points. Colm could sense the energy of the crowd shifting. The Gaeltacht fans were getting nervous. The Crokes fans were starting to believe.

Then in the twenty-third minute, the Crokes started working the ball up Colm's flank. Vince played a sweet pass into Colm. He could sense that midfielder Eoin Brosnan was making a lung busting run up the centre of the pitch. Colm played a delicate pass into open space that Eoin could run on to. Eoin caught the ball and was clear on goal.

He buried his shot in the bottom corner. Goal for the Crokes! Colm looked up at the scoreboard and couldn't believe his eyes: 1-3 to 0-0. How was this happening?

Dara Ó Cinnéide eventually scored, but when the ref blew for half-time, An Ghaeltacht had a solitary point to their name.

Colm jogged into the dressing room, expecting the lads to be patting each other on the backs. Inside the mood was closer to a funeral.

'Those Gaeltacht lads are going to throw everything at us. They'll have the wind at their backs,' his brother Vince said. He looked all of the young players directly in the eye.

'You're going to have to dig deeper than you've ever dug before.'

Colm knew he couldn't let his brother down.

'They didn't rate us,' Coach Harry said. 'They do now. Let's finish the job!'

Vince was completely right about the Gaeltacht comeback. They stormed back into the game as soon as the second half resumed. Darragh Ó Sé was winning everything in the midfield, and within six minutes, Dr Crokes lead by a mere two points.

'C'mon, lads,' Vince shouted. 'We haven't been training since January so we could fall at the last hurdle.'

Slowly the Crokes regained control. Danny earned a free, which Roland converted to give them a bit of breathing room. Colm remembered all of that training that he had put in that year. He just found another gear. His teammates did, as well. An Ghael-tacht cut their lead to one but in the dying minutes of the game, the Crokes passed the ball around the pitch like they were the Brazil football team. They had thirty passes in a row before someone from the Gaeltacht touched the ball.

'They can't score if they don't have the ball, lads,' Connie shouted. The game drifted into injury time. The Crokes just needed to see out two minutes.

'Blow it up, ref, blow it up,' their fans shouted nervously from the terraces.

Then the ref blew the whistle. Dr Crokes were the champions of Kerry! The final score was 1–04 to 0–06. It wasn't pretty. Dr Crokes had scored just one point in the second half but it was the score that won the game.

There was all-out jubilation on the pitch as the

Crokes fans coming running out to embrace their heroes. The head of the Kerry county board gave the trophy to Roland. He made a speech and talked about that first training session, back in January.

'I asked you to believe, lads, and you did.'

They showered, put on their blazers and headed over to the clubhouse for the banquet. All of Killarney seemed to be in there.

'I lifted this cup when I was captain of East Kerry back in 1965,' Donal the selector said. 'But this is sweeter. This is my proudest moment in the GAA.'

Colm couldn't stay out too late. He had to be in school for 9am. He left the banquet with his parents at 11pm. He put his medal underneath his pillow, and tried to sleep, but he couldn't. There was no point even trying. He just closed his eyes and played the match back in his head, over and over and over.

Just he before ran out the door the next morning, Vince called for him.

'Colm, I have something for you,' Vince said. He ran upstairs. He came down with the Bishop Moynihan Cup.

'Mind this for us today, would you?' he said. 'Take this with you and show it around the Sem.'

Colm couldn't believe it. Colm met Eanna at the entrance to the school, and they brought the trophy from classroom to classroom. They were legends. Just a year ago, he could barely get a game with the Kerry minor panel. Now he was a county champion. Colm knew if he never played another game of football, he'd already achieved something that so many Kerry footballers had failed to do. But he had no intention of hanging up his boots.

Colm Cooper was ready to kick on.

CHAPTER 14

COLM'S FIRST GAME IN CROKE PARK

It was a bright summer Sunday morning. Around Ireland, many people were going to mass. Meanwhile in Dublin, Colm walked inside the cathedral of the GAA – Croke Park – with his Kerry teammates. The Kerry minor team were getting familiar with the pitch ahead of the 2001 All-Ireland semifinal against Dublin later that afternoon.

'Good to be back,' Colm said to himself. It was nine years since he'd first set foot on this pitch. That day he was wearing the Dr Crokes mascot's tracksuit. Today, he was wearing that famous green and gold jersey of Kerry.

The game would kick off in just a few hours. Colm was starting at left corner forward. It was just as Colm had dreamed it all those years ago in Ardshanavooly.

They'd left Kerry on the train the previous afternoon, along with the Kerry senior team, who'd play the big match that day, the senior semi-final against Meath. On the trip up, Colm was too excited to be nervous. But that morning as the team bus crossed the River Liffey and drove up O'Connell Street, reality sank in. Colm was about to play in Croke Park.

Seeing it on television didn't do it justice: it was huge. The GAA had started renovation plans that would make it one of the biggest and most modern stadiums in Europe. As Colm ran, he named the four corners of the stadium in his own head.

In front of him was Hill 16. That's where the Dublin fans stood on their match days. To the left, the Hogan stand. That's where the All-Ireland-winning team would lift the cup and collect their medals. To the right, the Cusack stand, named after Michael Cusack, the founder of the GAA. Finally the Davin Stand at the Canal End, where Kerry warmed up.

Now that Colm was a little bit older, he could appreciate just how amazing it was to walk and play on the Croke Park pitch. The stadium was quiet and empty now, but soon it would be thronged with thousands of supporters. So many memorable Irish sports moments had happened on this pitch he and his teammates were walking on.

Colm hoped he'd get his chance to make some famous moments of his own.

Over the last season, Colm's idea of himself as a footballer had changed. No longer was he just a Dr Crokes player. He was an established Kerry footballer at minor level. He'd been training for more than a year with the Kerry minors. He'd started both games of Kerry's Munster campaign that year, and had made the left corner forward position his own. He'd kicked 1-3 as Kerry routed Waterford in the Munster semi-final. Then he'd scored two points as the Kerry minors beat Cork in the Munster final in Páirc Uí Chaoimh in Cork to become Munster minor champions for 2001.

The reward for a Munster title was an All-Ireland semi-final against the Leinster champions Dublin in Croke Park.

'Keep going like this and you might be playing for the Kingdom in a few years,' some supporters would tell him. Colm knew it was important to stay grounded.

All his life he'd heard about brilliant footballers who'd been savage at minor level, but never kicked on to enjoy intercounty success.

'You need to enjoy every moment of it, Colm, because sport is a funny business,' his dad told him before he left for the bus.

Colm remembered his father's words as he walked around the empty pitch. He tried to let as much of it soak in as possible. The huge pockets of green space, the Ard Chomhairle in the Hogan Stand, and of course Hill 16.

The reward of winning today would mean another trip back to Dublin in a few weeks time, to play in the All-Ireland final.

'Ask any footballer or hurler in this country to tell you about their first match played in Croke Park, and they'll tell you everything in great detail,' their coach Charlie said. 'Remember this, fellas. It's one of the greatest things a GAA player will ever experience.'

Colm was the only Dr Crokes player in the Kerry fifteen to start against Dublin. He'd grown quite close to the other players in the minor panel. There was the makings of a great team here. With himself and Declan, Kerry had one of the best full forward lines of any minor team in the country. Their goalie was a lad named Bryan Sheehan from Cahirsiveen who could kick the ball farther than any player Colm had ever known.

There were also a few interesting 'diamonds in the rough', as his dad called them. There was a lad from Tralee named Kieran Donaghy, a big, tall midfielder, who had represented Ireland in basketball at underage level. He was first and foremost a basketball player, but he had so much raw athletic potential, if only the management could figure out how to use him. He was a great character as well. A bit of a rogue, as he liked to say himself!

There was so much talent coming through in Kerry. Optimism was high in the county. They were the reigning All-Ireland champions at senior level. After so many bad years in the late 1980s and 1990s, there was a feeling in the county that Kerry were on the cusp of a new era.

Dublin had a very good team, and Colm knew this was probably the most important game he'd ever played in his life. But he didn't let the pressure take away from the amazing feeling of playing at Croke Park. Playing minor games in Croke Park was a strange experience because most of the fans wouldn't arrive until the second half, ahead of the senior game. When the ball was up at the other edge of the pitch, he'd look around in amazement at the massive stadium. The crowd was arriving slowly and any time he shouted for the ball, his voice echoed.

When he found a bit of space with the ball beneath the Hogan Stand, he took a brief look up at the goal posts. He struck the ball sweetly towards Hill 16 and it cleared the goal posts. When the umpire raised the white flag, he knew he'd done something he could tell his grandkids about. He'd scored a point in Croke Park.

The Dubs won the match 2-13 to 2-9. Colm scored two points but it wasn't enough. When the referee blew the final whistle, Colm felt incredibly disappointed. It was his last game at minor level. Kerry had aspired to win the All-Ireland and they'd fallen short.

They showered, changed and went back out to watch the senior team play their semi-final against Meath. The Royal County had been one of the best teams of the last decade and they completely blitzed Kerry. It finished up 2-14 to 0-5. It was one of Kerry's worst ever performances in Croke Park. The Kerry supporters were massively disappointed and they let the players and their manager Páidí Ó Sé know all about it.

Colm could hear all of the criticism from his seat beside the Kerry bench. He knew Páidí could hear it took but he acted like he didn't notice it.

The train ride home felt about ten hours long.

'It's different in Kerry,' Colm's dad said when he got home. 'We expect All-Ireland's every year, whether it's senior or minor. For a lot of the supporters, it's a lost year.'

CHAPTER 15

COLM MEETS PÁIDÍ

Eighteen is the age people go from being considered a child to being considered an adult.

As an eighteen-year-old, Colm was like most other lads his age. He liked to hang around Killarney with his mates. He liked to listen to Westlife and Boyzone. He liked to watch the Premier League. He liked to argue who the best striker in the Premier League was. Some said Arsenal's Thierry Henry. Others said Manchester United's Ruud van Nistelrooy. Colm was a Liverpool fan and knew it was Liverpool's Michael Owen.

But Colm was different from the other lads in some important ways. Even in the dead of winter, his focus was football. He spent a lot of evenings at the Dr Crokes pitch, kicking 45s or working on his touch, kicking off his left and his right.

Some of his friends moved to Limerick or Cork or Dublin for university, but Colm loved Killarney and was happy to stay home. He worked and when the working day ended, his thoughts returned to football. It was all he cared about. Even after the club went out of the Kerry championship, he'd be down at Dr Crokes, training on his own. He still lived at home with his parents in Ardshanavooly and all that mattered to him was becoming the best footballer he could be.

One November night while training at the club, Colm was approached by Pat, one of the coaches from the senior team.

'Gooch, I got a phone call from the county board today,' Pat said. 'Páidí Ó Sé might be in touch to ask you to link up with the Kerry senior team.'

'Are you joking?' Colm said.

'I am not!' Pat said. 'He asked for your mobile number. Word travels fast in Kerry. He must know how good you've been playing for us.'

Colm laughed off the idea that Páidí Ó Sé was serious about bringing him into the Kerry team.

But he was nervous about the phone call. Páidí was Kerry royalty. He was a larger than life figure and one of the most famous men in the GAA. He'd won eight All-Ireland's with Kerry as a player and two as manager. He owned a world famous pub on the Dingle peninsula. Movie stars like Tom Cruise had visited there.

'They don't make men like Páidí Ó Sé any more,' Colm's dad said. 'He's some character.'

One afternoon, Colm was in Cork and his mobile rang. He didn't recognise the number. He wondered if he should answer it. After a few rings, he did.

'Is this Colm Cooper?' The voice on the other end of the line had a strong west Kerry accent.

'It is,' Colm said.

'Hello, young Cooper,' Páidí said. 'Or can I call you The Gooch? It's Páidí Ó Sé.'

'Hello, Mr Ó Sé,' Colm said'

'Ah please, I'm Páidí, though lots of people call me PO,' he said. 'Here now, Gooch, word of your phenomenal performances with Dr Crokes and the Kerry minors has reached us down on the Dingle peninsula. The lads will be kicking off winter training soon. We want to give you a shot in a few challenge matches with the seniors.'

'Ok.'

'Nothing too serious, now. No pressure. We just want to ease you into the system and get a feel for the pace of intercounty football. One of Kerry's greatest forwards Maurice Fitzgerald retired, as you know. We badly need to replenish our forward line.'

'I'll give it my best, Páidí.'

'That's what I like to hear. And do one thing for me, would you?'

'Sure. What's that?'

'Have a few extra spuds with dinner tonight – you're gonna need to add on a few pounds if you're going to be playing for Kerry!'

'I will, of course, Páidí!' Colm said.

Colm couldn't wait to tell his family the good news. It felt a bit like Christmas Eve at the dinner table that night. A few of his brothers and sisters called in to celebrate the news. They were giddy. Colm would always be the little brother in the family, but his siblings looked at him a bit differently that night.

'Eighteen and playing county football, not bad

Colm, not bad at all,' Danny said.

His mother was very quiet throughout the dinner.

'What do you think about it all, Mam?' Colm said

'I'm not sure, Colm,' she said. 'Do you think it might be a bit soon to be playing with the Kerry team? There's some big lads you'll be coming up against.'

'He can handle himself, Maureen,' Colm's dad said, with a smile.

'Don't worry, Mam. I'll be fine. Trust me,' Colm said. 'You can't say no to Kerry.'

Colm's mother laughed.

'I have full faith in you,' she said, before serving him three more potatoes. 'You'll just need to eat a lot more of these this winter.'

'Páidí Ó Sé said as much,' Colm said.

CHAPTER 16

COLM WITH THE KERRY TEAM

The first challenge match that Colm took part in that season took place on a dark night in late January. Colm was one of forty players in attendance, the best footballers the county had to offer.

'Our goals are simple, lads,' Páidí Ó Sé said. 'We beat Cork or Limerick to win Munster. And whoever is left to win the All-Ireland. But I tell you one thing, those Northern teams, the likes of Armagh and Tyrone, are coming for us. And we better be ready.'

The Ó Sé family had a massive presence in the team. Páidí was manager and three of his nephews were also likely to be in Kerry's starting fifteen that year. There was Darragh Ó Sé, a rock in midfield and captain of the team, his brother Tomás, one of the best young halfbacks in the country, and Marc, who was then only twenty-three, but seemed certain to be a fixture in the Kerry backline for years.

'Welcome to the panel,' Dara Ó Cinnéide, one of the most established players, said to him after that first training session.

'Any advice for this whippersnapper, Dara?' Tomás said.

'When Páidí's your manager, be ready for anything!'

Colm had remembered how thrilled he was to beat the Ó Sé's and Dara back in the county final two years ago. Now they were teammates. For Colm, it was like being around celebrities. He looked at the likes of Seamus Moynihan and Eamonn Fitzmaurice, two Kerry legends, and wondered if it was all a dream!

Colm's main goal was not to do anything that would make him stand out or embarrass himself. He didn't want Páidí to change his mind about inviting him in! Early season training was all about fitness. They ran. A lot. Behind the scenes, he knew the selectors were having serious conversations about how Kerry would build a challenge and take back Sam Maguire.

Colm played with the Kerry 'B' team in the training matches, which meant being marked by county's best defenders. He knew he had so much growing to do. But he didn't feel massively out of his depth at this level. Even though he was skinny, he was strong under the highball. He was as good with his right foot as he was with his natural left foot. These were the raw skills that every forward needed to succeed. Defenders took him for granted because he looked like a kid, that was their problem.

The months passed, the ground hardened, the days got longer.

The league campaign had gone well for Kerry. Even though he wasn't in the match day squad for the league games, he felt like he played some role in the positive results. Colm was training with the Kerry U21s at that same time and he felt much more comfortable at that level. But he was learning so much from being around the senior team.

Kerry had reached the 2002 League 2 final against Laois in Limerick. That last week of training was vital for everyone in the squad, but not just because of the match. After the league final, the squad would break up for a few weeks and the Championship squad would be named. This training session would be one of Colm's last chances to impress Páidí and the selectors.

'You know what?' Colm said at dinner one night. 'I think I have an outside chance of making the Kerry panel for the summer.'

'With the form you're in, I'd believe it,' Vince said.

The Kerry U21s were his main priority, but Colm had a hunch – and it was only a hunch – that Páidí might keep him involved for the summer. He hadn't been in any Kerry teams for the league campaign, but he gave the defenders a real test in training in those As vs Bs games.

The night before the final training session before the League final, Colm received a phone call. He recognised the number this time. It was Páidí.

'Colm, PO here. Listen. I want you to know that you'll be starting on Sunday in the League final. I've every confidence in you.'

'Ok, Páidí,' Colm said. He was shocked by the news.

And with that he hung up the phone. Colm was in shock, he'd never played a single match with the Kerry A team. He wondered how the established players in the Kerry forward line – the All-Ireland winners! – would react.

Colm trained with Kerry the next night, and after the session, Páidí called the team into a huddle. The older players surrounded their manager, while Colm hung towards the back of the group

'Lads, I have the team for the league final here,' he said, holding up a piece of paper. 'Gooch Cooper, step forward.'

Colm humbly raised his hand.

'Gooch, I'm starting you at right corner forward.'

Colm could feel himself blushing

'We're building for the Championship,' Páidí said. 'I'm going to blood some new players on Sunday.

'I'll be ready, Páidí,' Colm said.

'Good man, Colm,' Darragh said. 'No bother to you.'

It was encouraging to get the backing of the captain. But Colm still felt uncomfortable. He could see some of the other players looked surprised by the news. Colm had never played for Kerry before.

Now he was starting in a league final. Okay, it wasn't Croke Park or the All-Ireland final but there was silverware on the line. Colm was still just 18.

'You have nothing to lose, Colm,' Vince said to him after training.

Colm agreed, but he just couldn't get his head around it. On the day of the match, he had his dad drive him to the ground thirty minutes before everyone else. He wanted to be the first one there.

On the bus, Páidí was barking orders like a drill sergeant. He'd never seen such an inspirational coach.

'Lads, prepare for the worst weather today. Hailstones and all. Everyone in gloves and long sleeve jerseys. And remember when you're out there. You're playing for Kerry. The green and gold.'

Colm only had one pair of gloves. They were big and black and looked like peat briquettes. The Kerry jersey they'd given him was about three sizes too big for him. He was going to have to make do.

Darragh lead the Kerry team in the parade. Colm wore number 15 and brought up the parade, as was tradition. 'Is this really happening?' Colm asked himself as he walked behind All-Ireland winners

Liam Hassett and Mike Frank Russell. Now he had something in common with the Kerry greats, like Mick O'Connell and Mick O'Dwyer and Jack O'Shea. They had all worn the green and gold jersey of Kerry in a senior game.

The ref threw the ball in. Tomás played a ball up the line, right to Colm. He started soloing towards the Laois goal, and left his marker behind with a little juke. Colm expected the Laois defence to converge on him, so he sprinted with all of his speed. Next thing he knew, he was one-on-one with the Laois keeper.

'Go for a goal, Gooch!' Colm heard Páidí shout.

So he did. Colm shot for the bottom right corner. To Colm's amazement, the shot beat the keeper and landed in the back of the net.

'Goal for Colm Cooper the debutante! His teammates call him the Gooch!' the commentator on Radio Kerry shouted. 'With his first touch of the ball in a Kerry jersey! Have you ever seen anything like it?'

Colm couldn't believe it. Neither could his marker by the look of things: he was shouting blue murder and looked ready to kill somebody. Colm prepared himself for some heavy defending.

The next time a high ball came in to the forward line, Colm's marker took him out of it. They wrestled on the wet ground until the ref stopped play. Colm's marker had given him a serious dig in the ribs and pulled his shirt up over his head.

'Behave yourself, lads, you're big boys,' the ref shouted.

Off the free, Colm broke into space. A pass came into him and he quickly shot it over the bar.

'Gooch!' Páidí shouted, pointing right at him.

Colm started to sprint for the bench, thinking he was being subbed off.

'No, no, son,' Paudi shouted. 'Your jersey. It's on the wrong way around.'

Colm looked down at himself. His jersey was on back to front and he didn't even notice. It must have happened during the scrap with the Laois cornerback.

'Thanks!' Colm said, and fixed his shirt.

When the ref blew the final whistle, Kerry won 1-9 to 1-5. Colm had finished with 1-2 to his name.

'Your 1-2 was the difference between winning and extra time,' Tomás said. 'So we owe you.'

Darragh went up on stage to collect the trophy and gave a very short speech. It was not the Kerry way to go wild about a league title. But it was the biggest day in Colm's career as a footballer.

CHAPTER 17

COLM EARNS HIS PLACE

The next week, Colm received a phone call from Pa, one of the selectors.

'You've been named in the Championship squad,' Pa said. 'Well done, Gooch, you've earned your place.'

Not only was Colm being included in the senior panel for the 2002 Championship, he had a chance of playing regularly if he continued in this form.

'Páidí's looking to freshen up the forward line and you've got all the raw skills to make it,' Pa said.

The Championship opener was against Limerick in two months. Colm was over the moon. But he was nervous, as well. Intercounty fullbacks were going to see him as a pushover. One particularly rough night in training, Colm was knocked around by Seamus Moynihan, one of the best Kerry defenders of all time. He stepped right on the scale in the family bathroom as soon as he got home.

'Ten stone,' Colm said to his dad. 'I'm going to get battered out there.'

'There's all kinds of footballers,' his dad said. 'But if you don't play to your strengths, you'll never get anywhere.'

His dad was right. Colm might not have been strongest player in the Kerry panel but he had other skills. He was phenomenal under the high ball. He was over six foot at age eighteen and he was still growing. With the ball in hand, he was difficult to stop. He had vision. His touch with his left boot was fantastic.

And best of all, he was unknown. All the die-hards in Kerry football knew about 'The Gooch' but in Limerick, Cork and Tyrone, people had no idea who he was.

'Here's what we're going to do, lads,' Páidí said at training before the first Championship match of the year. 'Backs, when you break from defence, drive it long and high into the full forward line.

'The likes of Gooch here will create havoc under the high ball, and Mike Frank, you can hoover it up after it breaks.'

This was the Kerry way of playing. Kicked passes, high fielding, and most importantly, stylish forward play.

'They see something in you, Colm,' his brother Mike told him. 'They know what we've known all along!'

CHAPTER 18

COLM'S FIRST
ALL-IRELAND FINAL

Colm woke up in the Tara Towers hotel, along the Dublin seaside. He looked out the window at the green Irish Sea.

'Today is the day,' he said to his roommate Ronan, another up-and-coming player with the Kerry team.

It was the day of the All-Ireland final. Kerry were playing Armagh. Nineteen-year-old Colm 'Gooch' Cooper was starting at right corner forward.

Colm was under strict instructions to shower and join the team for breakfast in a half hour. That gave Colm just enough time to reflect on just how mad

COLM'S FIRST ALL-IRELAND FINAL

of a season it had been.

By any measure, Colm's first season with the Kerry senior team had gone brilliantly. He'd kept his place in the starting team after the league final against Laois. He'd been subbed before half-time in the Munster final against Cork, which Kerry drew. He started the replay, which Kerry lost. All in all, it was a tremendous experience. He'd played Kerry's ancient rivals twice. Once in Fitzgerald Stadium, which practically his back garden, and the other time in Cork.

In the qualifiers, Colm really found his groove. He scored his first Championship goal against Fermanagh in the second round of the qualifiers. Then he added 1-1 against Kildare the next week out and was named Man of the Match for the first time as a senior intercounty player. Then came four points from play in the quarterfinal against the reigning All-Ireland champions Galway. Finally Colm scored a remarkable 1-5 in the All-Ireland semi-final, as Kerry got their revenge on Cork with a 15-point hammering. Colm had 3-13 to his name in his first Championship season, with the All-Ireland final still to play.

It wasn't just people in Kerry: the whole country was now talking about 'The Gooch', the gangly red-head with the golden touch. Pundits and experts couldn't understand how a player who looked so slight and skinny could be so effective in front of goal. He looked like a boy amongst very big men, but Colm was never intimidated or overwhelmed.

'You'll have an X on your back today,' Ronan said. 'Those Armagh boys will be looking to stop you.'

Colm knew, and he was ready. He'd weighed himself during the week. He was still 10 stone! He'd need to muster every ounce of strength he had to fight off the Armagh defenders today.

Colm and Ronan try to keep their head down when they entered the lobby. The hotel was swarming with Kerry supporters wearing green and gold.

It had been a crazy few weeks since winning the semi-final. It was much different from going for a county title with Dr Crokes. The phone was ringing off the hook at his home place. Distant cousins were calling the house asking for spare All-Ireland tickets. The whole county was buzzing for the match, and they were all talking about him, 'The Gooch'.

'Go on, Gooch!' strangers would shout at him as

he walked down the street. He stopped going to the supermarket with his mam because it was less hassle for everyone.

Colm couldn't get over how fast it had all happened. Some players like the Ó Sés grew up knowing they would someday play in All-Ireland finals for Kerry. Colm had only just broken into Kerry development squads two years ago. Now he was set to start an All-Ireland final at just nineteen years of age.

Before he headed to training on the Tuesday before the final, he headed out to the Ardshan green for a kick about with the younger kids in the estate. It was great to remember the game he'd be playing on Sunday against Armagh was the same game he'd learned here.

The estate took such pride in having a player in the Kerry team. Each of the 120 houses in the estate had a Kerry flag hanging outside its front door that week. Some had two.

The conventional wisdom was that Kerry were hot favourites to win. Colm picked up a few newspapers on the journey up. 'Game of two haves: the haves and the have-nots' one headline read.

The Orchard County had never won an All-Ireland before. Kerry had won thirty-two.

Kerry's full forward line was in fantastic form. Between himself, Mike Frank and Dara, they'd scored 6-60 over the Championship. But Armagh had some ferocious defenders.

'Be ready. You've never seen tacklers like these Northern boys,' Mike Frank said on the train up. The likes of Kieran McGeeney, Francie Bellew and the McNulty brothers were seen as some of the best backs in the country.

Even though the bookies had Kerry as big favourites, Páidí and the Kerry players were preparing everyone for an onslaught. Armagh had pushed Kerry to the brink two years earlier, drawing the 2000 All-Ireland semi-final and the replay before losing in extra time.

Colm could really feel the butterflies in his stomach as the team bus pulled into Croke Park.

'Just take deep breaths and don't let the occasion get to you,' Páidí said to him before he began warming up.

Colm tried to remember every little detail of the day. Kerry warmed up in the Canal End of Croke

Park, as they did traditionally. It was an honour to shake the hand of President Mary McAleese – it was the first time he had met the President! The parade was everything he expected it to be. The noise in the stadium was deafening, he could barely hear the Artane Band. The Armagh supporters and Kerry supporters brought so much colour and emotion. He tried to only think about the match, but it was nice to remember that somewhere in that crowd of 80,000 were his parents and siblings, cheering for him. They were probably more nervous than he was. Colm would try his best not to let them down.

After the anthems, he knew it was time to get down to business.

Kerry started the game brilliantly. Colm was being marked by Enda McNulty, a ferocious man-marker but Colm was slippery. He wriggled away to create an early score for Mike Frank. Armagh couldn't live with the pace of the Kerry attack. A ball broke right in Colm's path in front of goal.

'Point or goal?' he asked himself very quickly. He played the percentages and kicked it over the bar.

'Keep that scoreboard ticking over, Gooch!' Mike Frank said. Kerry led by three at half time. Colm had two scores to his name.

'We're close enough to taste it, lads,' Darragh said, back in the dressing room. 'Thirty-five more minutes like that and it's won.'

But a different Armagh team came out in the second half. They were flying into tackles like their lives depended on it. Oisín McConville scored a goal on the counterattack and the momentum swung totally against Kerry.

'C'mon, lads,' Colm shouted at the other forwards, but it made no difference.

Armagh took the lead and didn't give it up. The final score was 1-12 to 0-14. Kerry couldn't defend their four point lead. They only managed three points in the second half, and just one from play. The Armagh fans stormed the pitch the second the final whistle blew. Colm had never seen pandemonium like it in his life.

He was gutted afterwards. His family consoled him at the post-match banquet.

'You'll get more chances, Colm,' his brother Mike said. 'Don't take it too hard.'

'Exactly. You scored two points in the All-Ireland final,' Geraldine said. 'Not many people can say that.'

Colm agreed. But it wasn't just emotional pain. He was still feeling worse for wear after a hard challenge from Kieran McGeeney. Colm knew he'd have to get stronger to play with the big boys.

Thousands of Kerry supporters attended the homecoming in Killarney the next day. The whole team were gutted to lose the All-Ireland but it was inspiring to see so many supporters turn out. It made him want to win the All-Ireland not just for him and his teammates, but for the whole county.

A few weeks after the season ended, he picked up the newspaper to find out he'd been nominated for an All-Star. There so many brilliant forwards nominated that Colm knew he had no chance of winning. Still he rented a tuxedo and travelled up to Citywest for the gala awards evening.

He was shocked to learn he'd be chosen as All-Star at left corner forward. It was like winning an Oscar! He and Darragh Ó Sé were the only Kerry players to win All-Stars that year.

It was an incredible honour to be chosen as an All-Star at just nineteen. He was one of the youngest All-Stars ever. But all that winter, Colm only thought about one thing: getting back to Croke Park.

CHAPTER 19

KERRY DISCOVER THE POWER OF TYRONE

I t was August 2003, or the business end of the Championship, as the pundits all described it. Kerry had reached the All-Ireland semi-final. Their opponents would be Tyrone.

That winter, he realised just how famous inter-county footballers were in Kerry. Every time he walked down the street in Killarney, people recognised him.

Some people would salute him. Others would shake his hand. Some people would say hello like they'd known him for their whole life.

Kerry were aspiring to win their 33rd All-Ireland,

and things were looking up. Colm won his first Munster title that season. They'd defeated Limerick in the final in Fitzgerald Stadium 1-11 to 0-9.

It was a brilliant feeling to lift the Munster cup in his own home town.

'We'd have preferred if it was Cork,' Colm's dad said after the game, 'but a cup is a cup!'

Winning Sam Maguire in 2003 would involve beating the best of Ulster. Tyrone, Armagh and Donegal were the other semi-finalists. Tyrone were up first for Kerry.

Kerry had a funny relationship with the Northern counties. Northern teams approached Kerry differently. Colm had seen first-hand that some counties were intimidated by the green and gold jersey. But the Northern teams like Armagh and Tyrone seemed to get bigger and faster when they saw the green and gold jersey.

Colm also learned that Kerry supporters didn't really appreciate the Ulster tactics.

'Ah, those Northern counties are very difficult to watch,' a man in the town said to him one day.

'You wouldn't be begrudge them the success, but it's a bad brand of football.'

The Northern philosophy to football was different to the Kerry traditional way of playing. It was low-scoring and often defensive, win at all cost.

'You have to understand, Colm,' his father had told him. 'Up north, they approach the game differently. They think the likes of us down here in Kerry don't respect them as footballers.'

'But those Armagh lads and those Tyrone lads are all fabulous footballers. They've just discovered a style that suits them better. And most importantly, their style is harder to stop by playing our traditional game.'

Colm agreed. Tyrone had some truly class footballers. They had one of the best forwards of all time in their team, Peter Canavan. The semi-final would be Colm's first Championship playing against the man they called 'Peter the Great'.

It had been a tough season for Colm. He'd kept his place in the full-forward line, but he'd been slowed down by a groin injury he couldn't shake. The team doctor said he had a torn adductor muscle and it could require surgery. Colm decided he'd play through it and see what happened.

Páidí had prepared Kerry reasonably well for the

semi-final and the whole Kerry team were confident when they left Killarney for Dublin. They all thought losing last year's All-Ireland final against Armagh had set them up well. As long as Kerry could play their game for seventy minutes and not drift out in the second half, like they had against Armagh, Tyrone would be in trouble.

But as soon as the ref threw the ball in, Colm realised Kerry were in for a rude awakening. Tyrone played like an agitated pack of wasps, swarming on the ball from every corner.

'It's like there's thirty Tyrone players playing,' Mike Frank said to him.

There were white jerseys everywhere. In his short career, Colm had never come up against like it on the football pitch.

'Pass, lads, pass!' Colm shouted, pleading with the backs. But they couldn't get the ball forward.

The Tyrone players were harrying like their lives depended on it. They didn't seem so bothered with scoring either. Their first priority was to disrupt Kerry. It was closer to a demolition derby than a football match.

Ten minutes into the match, Colm's clubmate

Eoin Brosnan found himself surrounded by eight Tyrone players – more than half the Tyrone team around one man! He was trying his hardest to get the ball to a teammate, but it was no use. At every direction he turned, he hit a brick wall.

'Just wait them out, they'll burn themselves out,' Colm thought.

But Tyrone never got tired. If anything Tyrone seemed to gain strength from watching the Kerry players get frustrated. Colm had never played against a team this fit and hungry in his life.

It took twenty-five minutes for Colm to kick Kerry's first point.

Colm clapped and tried to rile his teammates after the umpire raised the white flag, but that was the hardest Kerry had ever worked for a point.

Colm had never been happier to hear a full-time whistle in his life. The final score was 0–13 to 0–6. Kerry had lost. Six points! You might expect that from a league game in the middle of February played against an Atlantic squall, but not on a fine Sunday in August.

'Six points in an All-Ireland semi-final,' Dara

said in the dressing room. 'It's just not right.'

Páidí was stunned. It was one thing to lose, but Páidí was very proud. It hurt him to lose like this.

Kerry supporters were disgusted by the match. Pat Spillane called Tyrone's tactics 'puke football' on RTÉ. No one could remember a team playing like this before.

For all the outrage, Colm knew that Tyrone were deserving winners. And he wasn't surprised when Tyrone beat Armagh a few weeks later in the first All-Ireland final between two Ulster counties.

Tyrone were better conditioned, and most importantly, they had a better plan than Kerry.

'They don't just hand out All-Irelands, you have to go and win them,' Páidí had said earlier that year. He was right.

Colm had learned that the hard way after just two seasons with the Kerry team.

CHAPTER 20

KERRY LOSE AN UNLIKELY MATCH

'You'll remember your defeats much more than your victories,' Dara had said to him on the train down after the Tyrone match.

Dara had seen all the highs and lows of being a Kerry star, so Colm listened closely and remembered this words.

And they came back to him a few weeks later when the Kerry U21s were playing Waterford in the Munster final in Walsh Park in Waterford. Colm and Declan were starting among the forwards. Their coach Jack O'Connor had told them never to underestimate anyone, and the lads all agreed.

But Waterford had never won a Munster U21 title and Kerry were Kerry.

Waterford threw the kitchen sink at Kerry in the first half, and Kerry were rattled. Colm played decently, scoring three points from play, and though Kerry trailed at half-time, it seemed like they would find a way to win. Jack threw in Kieran Donaghy, the basketball player, off the bench, and Kerry held a two point lead into injury time.

Then, in the first minute of injury time, out of nowhere, Waterford scored a goal. Walsh Park erupted. All of a sudden, Kerry trailed. Moments later, the final whistle came. It was their worst nightmare. Kerry had been defeated by Waterford.

Colm put his hands over his head.

'We won't be allowed back in Kerry,' Kieran said.

These crushing defeats were getting too familiar. Colm wasn't even twenty-one yet and he'd already learned first-hand how cruel the game could be.

He decided to get surgery that winter for his groin injury. As he recovered, he decided one thing. Nothing was going to stop him from winning an All-Ireland next season.

CHAPTER 21

ALL-IRELAND GLORY

When the 2004 season arrived, Colm Cooper told himself one thing: 'this is my year.' He told himself that throughout the whole season: when Kerry won Munster, when Kerry beat Derry in the semi-final, and on the journey up to Dublin take on Mayo in the 2004 All-Ireland final.

He focused on himself because there was a lot to get hung up on in the county.

The loss to Tyrone the previous year had really stung Kerry GAA fans. 'The Kerry Way' that Páidí and Colm's dad would talk about wasn't enough to beat the Northern counties. Some Kerry fans wondered if their players were tough enough.

Páidí had quit as Kerry manager that winter.

Kerry had a new coach now: Jack O'Connor, who'd coached Colm with the U21s.

Jack was very different from Páidí. Jack wasn't part of the famous generation of Kerry players. He'd also managed Declan as a teenager.

'You guys are the future of Kerry football, you're both only twenty-one,' Jack had told Colm and Declan after the first training session. 'And we're building the team around you.'

Colm won his second Munster title that year. The draw had been kind to them at the business end of the season, and they got some luck along the way as well. Tyrone and Armagh had been knocked out in the quarterfinals. Kerry defeated Derry in the semifinal by 6 points. Now only Mayo stood between Colm and his first Sam Maguire.

'This Mayo team won't lie down for you. They want this badly,' Jack said in the dressing room on All-Ireland final day. 'Do you want it more than them? Hunger will win this All-Ireland for us.'

Mayo hadn't won an All-Ireland since 1951, and their fans were starved of success. It was different for Colm and Kerry. They had a point to prove to themselves.

The build-up to this All-Ireland final was different. In 2002, Colm just felt lucky to be there. But he'd learned how much losing big games hurt. He was bigger now and stronger too. If he had to, he'd win this All-Ireland on his own.

During the warm-ups, Colm spotted Mayo's two bleach-blond forwards, Conor Mortimer and Ciaran McDonald, kicking points. They were seen as two of the best forwards in the country. Colm knew they had serious talent.

'You'll show them who the best forward in the country is today, Gooch,' he heard a voice say in his ear. It was Paul Galvin, a young lad from North Kerry who had broken into the Kerry team that year. He played in the half forward line. He was fierce in defence and attack, like a Rottweiler.

Colm laughed, but he knew Paul was right. To be the best, first you had to think you were the best.

Colm knew Mayo would need to play the game of their lives to stop them on this day. Even when Mayo's Alan Dillon scored an early goal, Colm remained confident.

'I just need one clean ball,' he said to himself.

It took Kerry ten minutes or so to get a grip

of the game, but once they did, they didn't relent. Jack's strategy was brilliant: bomb high balls into the full forward line and see how the Mayo backs would cope.

After twenty-five minutes, Kerry had turned a four point deficit into a four point lead. Colm scored two points from play, both from scraps. He was still waiting for his moment to make a real impact on the game. Despite all of the noise in the stadium, Colm was calm. He sensed his moment was coming. And then he saw a ball coming in his direction from the other end of the pitch.

Eamonn Fitzmaurice had won a free around the Kerry 65. He played a huge ball into Colm. Gooch knew he was one-on-one with the Mayo wingback Pat Kelly. He knew without looking that the Mayo defence was napping and that there was an acre of space in front of goal.

Everything that happened next was like slow motion. Colm jumped up about seven feet in the air to collect the pass. He caught it cleanly and from the second he hit the ground, Colm's mind focused on going for goal. He stuck his arm straight – like an American football player – to create an angle for a run at goal.

Colm then blasted by his marker and turned towards the net. He was through. He hopped the ball off the ground once, then soloed with his left. A goal was on. Colm's easiest shot at goal was the near post, bottom right corner. But from the corner of his eye, he saw the Mayo cornerback charging into the open space to the right of goal.

He could also see the goalkeeper moving to cover that space.

Colm could feel all eighty thousand people in Croke Park rise to their feet in anticipation.

What would he do?

He did the one thing that no one expected. While the Mayo cornerback and goalie were certain Colm was going to rocket the ball into the bottom right corner, Colm sold them both a dummy. He stepped around the defence and calmly slotted the ball towards the bottom left corner with his left boot. He didn't need to watch the umpire raise the green flag. He closed his eyes and waited to hear the roar of the crowd.

And then the roar came, louder than anything he'd ever heard in his life.

It was Colm's first goal of the season, and it was worth waiting for.

'What poise! What skill! What a wonderful player! Absolute poetry in motion!' the commentator shouted on Radio Kerry. 'That's as wonderful a goal as I've ever seen on a football pitch.'

Colm released an almighty fist pump. Kerry lead by seven now. He knew this would be Kerry's day.

They went into half-time up eight points. In the dressing room, there was no complacency from the Kerry team. The losses to Armagh and Tyrone had toughened them up.

'Let's finish what we started,' Jack said. 'Play the second half like the scoreboard says nil-all.'

Mayo had a few chances to claw their way back in, but it made no difference. For Colm, it became like a training match. He pinged perfect passes across the pitch. He kicked points from impossible angles. Mayo tried different markers on him but it was no use. He was playing the game at a different speed to everyone else.

'Just watching him is worth the price of admission alone,' Martin Carney said on the RTÉ broadcast, paying Colm the highest compliment.

When the ref blew the full time whistle, Colm had 1–5 to his name. Kerry had scored 1–20 and won the 2004 All-Ireland title by eight points.

As he was celebrating with his teammates, a producer from RTÉ grabbed him.

'Gooch, you're Man of the Match, congratulations! Will you do an interview?'

'Sure!' Colm said.

In the minute it took to set the interview up, Colm looked across the pitch. Kerry people were invading from Hill 16 and the Hogan Stand. It was one of the most beautiful sights he'd ever seen.

'Colm Cooper,' the interviewer said. '1–4 from play and your first All-Ireland win. That was one of the greatest performances ever by a forward in an All-Ireland final. How does it feel?'

Colm paused and thought for a second about all the training sessions that winter. And the brutal defeats to Tyrone and Armagh. And the whole long struggle it took to break through with the Kerry team.

Colm smiled.

'It feels good,' he said, and smiled a massive smile. 'It feels REALLY good.'

CHAPTER 22

AN ALL-IRELAND
TO REMEMBER, AND FORGET

Colm was getting used to All-Ireland Sunday. In 2005, he again found himself in Dublin on the final Sunday of September, ready to play for Sam Maguire. This year, their opposition was Tyrone.

Throughout the build-up to the match, the media were asking the same questions: will Kerry have an answer to Tyrone's fierce defence?

There were a few reasons that Kerry fans were hopeful. For one, their legendary forward Peter Canavan had been carrying a serious knock. Peter was one of the best forwards of all time.

Also, the All-Ireland final would be Tyrone's tenth match of the Championship. Some people in Kerry thought this meant Tyrone would be exhausted for the All-Ireland. But Colm and his teammates knew better.

They knew Tyrone would be battle-hardened and ready for war.

Kerry's defence of the Sam Maguire had gone brilliantly. They were undefeated in the Championship. They beat Cork in the Munster final. To make things even better, they beat Cork in the All-Ireland semi-final.

Colm had been having a sensational season. All the papers were predicting he'd be voted Footballer of the Year if Kerry won the final.

But Jack had told the team what they already knew very well. Beating Tyrone would be a massive task. No team had ever played Gaelic football with that kind of hunger.

Colm still remembered how hurt he felt after Tyrone had beat Kerry in the 2003 semi-final – when Kerry had only scored six points. He was determined to prevent that from happening again.

In the second minute, Kerry won a free around

the 45. Colm raced into space. William Kirby played a pass into him. Colm had just enough space to steady himself. He turned and fired over a huge shot from about five feet from the sideline, from his left boot. It was a score of the highest class. Kerry fans rose to their feet to salute him. There was something magical about scoring the first point in an All-Ireland final.

Five minutes later, Paul played a hopeful long ball into the Kerry full forward line from midfield. Colm caught his marker napping and sprinted onto it. As he claimed the ball, he sensed Dara making a run towards goal. In one beautiful motion, he planted himself and fisted the ball over his shoulder, right into Dara's hands. Dara did the rest. Point for Kerry. Now they were up three.

Tyrone would not give up, and Colm knew it. The Red Hand started to knuckle down and turn the match into a dogfight. In the middle of the first half, Colm was charging into the penalty box when the Tyrone goalie Pascal McConnell came running out at him. They collided and Pascal's glove ran right into Colm's eye. Colm was in serious pain.

'I can't see a thing,' Colm said to the physio.

'Your eye is swollen from the collision,' Mick the physio said. 'It's going to sting for a bit.'

The physio squirted some water in his eye, but it didn't make a massive difference. Colm could only see properly out of one eye. It was impossible to be effective with only eye. Colm didn't bother asking himself whether the goalie intended to hurt him. Tyrone played close to the line. It was what made them hard to beat.

As Colm struggled with his vision, Tyrone stormed ahead. In added time in the first half, Peter Canavan found space in the Kerry box to score a beautiful goal in front of the Hill. Tyrone led by a goal. Canavan was then subbed out to get some rest. He was reintroduced in the second half as Kerry staged a comeback.

The Tyrone fans and players found a huge lift in Peter's reintroduction. Minutes later, Peter scored one of the greatest points Colm had ever seen: a high, soaring shot from an impossible angle deep in the left corner of the pitch. It gave Tyrone a two point lead. That's why they called him Peter the Great.

There was great heart in this Kerry team though and they fought to the end. With seconds left in injury time, Kerry launched one final attack. Colm popped out to the 45 metre line to spark the attack. Colm played a 1–2 with Darragh Ó Sé. Colm could see a goal opportunity beginning to develop but before he could do anything, he was rugby-tackled to the pitch by Canavan. The ref allowed the game to play on. As Colm was on the ground, Kerry lost possession and the final whistle sounded seconds later.

As Tyrone fans flooded onto the pitch, Colm could only feel anger. It had been an incredible match – nothing like the 'puke football' seen in 2003 between the two counties – but that was no solace to the Gooch. He'd scored five points in defeat, but that's all it was. Five points in another defeat to Tyrone.

CHAPTER 23

A FAMILY TRAGEDY

A month after Kerry lost to Tyrone, Colm was been awarded with an All-Star. It didn't matter too much to Colm because Kerry hadn't won the All-Ireland. It was fun to put on a tuxedo and head to Citywest for the gala dinner. It took away some of the pain of losing the All-Ireland final.

Colm was also selected to play to represent Ireland in the International Rules series taking place in Australia that October. It was an amazing feeling to be chosen to travel across the world to represent your country with the best Gaelic footballers in the country. Although the thought of playing some of the best and toughest Aussie Rules players was intimidating. It was amateurs against professionals.

Some great Gaelic footballers like Jim Stynes had even moved to Australia to play Aussie Rules. Colm knew if he played well enough, some Aussie Rules teams might be interested in signing him.

Much of the Ireland teams early training sessions were focused on mastering the laws of the game. The rules were a mix of Gaelic football and Aussie Rules. They used the round Gaelic football and played on a rectangular GAA pitch. But tackling was allowed and marks were called for clean catches of high balls. Two extra goal posts were set up so players could score 'behinds'.

It was the trip of a lifetime. The first test was in Perth, the second test was in Melbourne. The International Rules series was the only opportunity Colm would ever get to be teammates with his direct county rivals. The team consisted of seven lads from the Tyrone team that had defeated Kerry and won the All-Ireland the previous season. There were also three Cork players on the team. The tour was a great opportunity to get to know the players who usually marked him in big games. They weren't much different from the Kerry lads it turned out.

It was a pity about the games! Ireland had won last

year's series in Ireland, and the Aussies were determined not let that happen again. When the games threw in, Colm learned quickly that the Australians wanted to wrestle, not play football. Even worse, the referees seemed happy to let things go. Ireland lost the first. In the second and final Test, Colm got concussed from a hard tackle and had to go off injured. Ireland lost the series on an aggregate score of 163–106. On the long flight home, Colm decided he was happy to stick with Gaelic football.

In many ways, Colm's life had changed enormously since he'd made his intercounty debut four years ago. He'd become one of the most recognisable people in the GAA. He had a great nickname which contributed to his fame. But Colm still lived in his parents' house in Ardshanavooly. He got a job in a bank and loved being at home with his family.

The pressure was always there. Kerry people would forget about the GAA during the autumn months. But once Christmas passed and the league kicked off, it was all people in Killarney talked about.

Kerry made a decent start to the league in 2006. They won four games in a row after losing their first game to Mayo. Jack was trying out some new players and seemed committed to finding a place for Kieran Donaghy in the team.

There was a bit of a buzz in the town during the first week of April. The Dubs were coming to Kerry that weekend for a league match. As much as Kerry relished the border battles with Cork or the challenge of playing Tyrone and Armagh, there was nothing quite like playing Dublin. Colm knew it. All his teammates knew it.

Colm's mind was almost entirely on Dublin that Monday before the match when a man he knew from the town named Patrick O'Sullivan hurried into the bank in a panic.

'Colm,' Patrick said. 'Your father has collapsed up the town.'

'What?' Colm said.

'He was working and the workers said he had a turn and fainted. It sounds serious.'

'Oh no,' Colm said.

Pat and Colm jumped in the car and drove to Colm's house to collect his mother and tell her the news. When they arrived at the shopping centre where Mike Cooper had been working, the paramedics were lifting a body into the ambulance.

A medic pulled him aside.

'I'm so sorry, Colm. Your father passed away a few minutes ago. It looks like he had a massive heart attack. We did everything we could to revive him. I'm so sorry.'

Colm hugged his mother as she cried. No one could make sense of it. It started as a normal Monday but now his father was gone forever. Colm didn't know what to say. It was the worst day of his life.

The wake and the funeral passed like a blur. Colm couldn't imagine his life without his father. He especially couldn't imagine playing Gaelic football without his father. His dad had been there every step of the way in Colm's career, from the first time he picked up a football to when he climbed up the Hogan Stand steps to lift Sam Maguire.

Nothing would be the same anymore. It was so unfair.

At the funeral, friends and family tried to talk to him about football to take his mind off the grief he felt. But football was the last thing he wanted to think about it. It just reminded him of his dad.

All of his teammates and coaches came to the

funeral to pay their respects. Colm really appreciated that. Jack had told him to sit out the Dublin
match. Colm was relieved.

A few nights before the Dublin match, Colm got
chatting to his mam.

'It just won't be the same without him in the
terraces,' Colm said. 'He was there for every match.'

'I know,' Colm's mam said. 'I've been thinking
more about it. He wouldn't want you missing a
Kerry match for any reason.'

Colm laughed. She was right.

'Playing against Dublin might be the best way to
remember him,' she said.

It made sense. His mind had been a million miles
away from the Gaelic football pitch, but maybe
football could relieve their pain, for a few hours
anyway.

Colm let Jack know he was available for selec-
tion. Jack thanked him and said he'd use him off
the bench, as a high-impact sub.

'Fifteen minutes would make a big difference for
us,' Jack said.

As he togged out and warmed up, Colm knew
he wasn't fully at the races. He was drained. He'd

barely slept that week. But there was something comforting about pre-match stretching drills. It help him forget.

Colm started the game from the bench, and had a great view of Dublin's domination. With fifteen minutes left in the game, and Dublin leading by two, Jack decided to introduce Colm.

'On for Kerry, Colm Cooper!' said the man over the tannoy.

There was a huge roar. Everyone in Kerry knew what had happened that week.

Colm had decided he wasn't going to let his family down. With his first touch of the ball, Colm turned and shot. The ball sailed over the bar. The Kerry fans cheered and shouted. Colm felt almost overcome with emotion. All the emotion and adrenaline passed through him. The match finished a draw.

During the warm down, Jack pulled the team aside.

'Great effort today, lads, and special credit to Gooch here for togging out.'

The whole Kerry squad started to clap. Even though he was a little embarrassed with the attention, he appreciated it so much. These guys weren't just his teammates, they were his brothers.

CHAPTER 24

CRISIS IN THE TEAM

A few months later, Kerry won the National League for the second year in a row. For Colm, all of the success of recent years came with a down side. Following the tactic employed by Tyrone, teams were now directly targeting him. They'd sometimes double mark him. They'd sometimes use cheap shots. Whatever it took to slow him down. 'Stop Gooch and you stop Kerry' was the mantra.

All of this made it next to impossible for Colm to play his own game.

It was a hard year for him. Football offered a bit of escape from the sadness of losing his beloved father, but his game suffered.

All of the Kerry team seemed to struggle with the pressure of having to win the All-Ireland back that year. Declan was Kerry captain that year and his game seemed off as well.

In June, Kerry drew with Cork in a wild Munster final in Killarney. The replay was the following week in Páirc Uí Chaoimh. Colm managed a solitary point in the first game, and he scored the same in the replay. Cork won the replay by six. It was a terrible match for Kerry. Even worse than the result, Declan had been booed by the Kerry supporters when he was subbed off. Colm couldn't believe his ears. Sure, Declan was having a poor game, but he was a great footballer who loved wearing the Kerry shirt.

They sat beside each other on the long bus ride back to Killarney after the defeat.

'We'll go again, don't worry,' Colm said. The result meant they'd play Longford in the qualifiers in six days.

'Longford are dangerous and you're all out of form. It's a dangerous game,' Vince said during the week.

Everyone was aware that something was wrong

with the Kerry attack. Kerry didn't score a single goal in the Munster championship. Gooch couldn't do everything on his own.

The next Tuesday in training, Jack pulled Colm aside.

'I have two pieces of news for you, Gooch,' Jack said. 'I'm dropping Declan for the Longford game. He's rattled. That means you're captain since Dr Crokes were runners up in the Kerry championship final last year.'

'Okay,' Colm said. 'What's the other news?'

'I have a plan for Longford. If it doesn't work I might be out of a job.'

'Let's hear it,' Colm said.

'See that big fella over there,' Jack said, pointing to Kieran Donaghy. 'I'm going to start him at full forward against Longford.'

Colm did a double take. Donaghy had never played full forward before. He played as a midfielder with club and county. His job was to break ball and win kick outs. Full forward was a different beast altogether.

'Can he play full forward though?'

'No, but we might be able to teach him.'

'We?' Colm said.

'We'll need your help, Colm. And we don't have much time. Longford are here in five days.'

Jack informed the team of his tactical idea. There were some raised eyebrows, but the players were open to the idea.

'It's crazy enough that it just might work,' Darragh said.

They played an As vs Bs game with Kieran in the full forward line. The backs were given one task: kick the ball high and long into Kieran.

When the first ball came in, Kieran leaped over three defenders, won the ball cleanly and offloaded to Colm. Gooch tapped in for an easy goal.

They learned two things in training that night.

The first that Kieran was almost unmarkable under the high ball. Basketball had taught Kieran how to turn his six foot five inch frame into a human shield.

The second thing that they'd discovered was Kieran had a lot to learn about the position. How to shoot, when to shoot, how to win a free, how to pass in closed spaces. Luckily Kieran was ready to learn.

'Teach me how to be The Gooch,' Kieran said to him after training that first night.

'I'm not sure I can do that,' Colm said. 'But I'll tell you everything I know.'

'That's good enough for me!' Kieran said.

CHAPTER 25

A STAR IS BORN

The next night, Kieran turned up in Ardshana-vooly. Colm grabbed a bag of footballs from the house and lead Kieran to the Ardshan green.

'Are we not going down to the GAA pitch?' Kieran asked.

'We have everything we need right here,' Colm said.

They walked over to the metal post that Colm had practised against when he was young.

'Being a good full forward starts with touch and accuracy,' Colm said. 'So take fifty shots off your left and fifty off your right. I'll collect the balls.'

It was the simplest exercise, but Kieran struggled with it. He was a basketball player at heart. He wanted to use his hands and elbows, but if he didn't develop touch with his feet he'd never make.

'One thing to always keep in mind,' Colm said. 'When you're one-on-one with the keeper, don't try to kill the keeper with the shot. Find the space where the keeper isn't and pass the ball into the net.'

Kieran nodded. He had a lot to learn, but Colm knew Kieran had the raw skills. If Donaghy could gain a bit of finesse, it would make Colm's life so much easier.

There was an uneasy feeling in Fitzgerald Stadium on the day of the Longford game.

The Kerry supporters had grown frustrated with their team that summer. Many of them were shocked at the idea of playing a basketball player at full forward. Only in Kerry, where people had such a high regard for their own footballing tradition, would this have been an issue.

The Donaghy experiment had to work, or else Jack had managed his last Kerry game.

Luckily, things couldn't have gone any better against Longford. Kieran was unstoppable. Sixteen minutes into the game, Kerry led 3-2 to 0-3. Kieran had set up all three of the Kerry goals, including one for Colm. Longford tried triple-marking Kieran but it made no difference. Kerry won 4-11 to 1-11 in the end.

No one benefited more than Colm. He scored 1-2 from play. Suddenly he was free to play his natural game.

'Donaghy stands tall as air raids put paid to plucky Longford', the *Irish Independent* read the next day.

After just one match, all of Kerry's woes had been forgotten. They were like new men.

There was only one problem. They'd play their old friends Armagh in the quarterfinals. Those Armagh boys wouldn't be caught out by Donaghy.

During the build-up to the match, and on the trip up, Colm's mind focused on one thing: hurt. He remembered how much it had hurt to lose in 2002 in Armagh. He especially remembered how much it had hurt to lose in 2003 and 2005 to Tyrone. He wasn't ready to make that long journey back to Kerry having been mugged by another team from Ulster.

In the back of Colm's mind, a small voice wondered if they would ever beat Armagh or Tyrone. He knew they needed to win this match in order to be considered a 'great team'.

Colm was Kerry captain for the quarterfinal. It usually wasn't his place to make passionate pre-match speeches – he left it to the older fellas and let his football do the talking. But Colm knew he couldn't let the lads out onto the pitch without saying something.

'Fellas, these Northern teams have bullied us in the past. That ends here, today. Those Armagh boys are about to see a Kerry team like no other.'

The Armagh backs wasted no time getting 'familiar' with Colm and Kieran. Kieran was being marked by Francie Bellew, who was probably the best defender in the game.

Bellew was especially physical marking Kieran. The high balls into Donaghy weren't sticking like they had in the Longford game. And the ref didn't have much sympathy for the roughhousing of Donaghy. He swallowed his whistle.

Kieran wasn't the kind of player to stay silent if he thought a ref got a call wrong. He flailed his hands at the ref.

'They're fouling me, ref!' Kieran shouted. 'His hands were all over me!'

The ref sprinted down the field, uninterested.

Another high ball came in to the Kerry forward line. Kieran and Bellew wrestled for it. Kieran was knocked off balance. Again the ref didn't blow for a free.

'Quit your whinging, cry-baby,' Paul Hearty their goalie shouted at Kieran as the action moved up field.

Colm could see that Kieran was getting frustrated. Armagh were clearing every high ball. Kieran was such an emotional guy, and he was trying so hard. But these Armagh defenders were street savvy. Up the other end of the pitch, the Armagh forwards were having their way with the Kerry backs.

Gooch approached Kieran.

'Listen, you need to be patient. We just need one goal to turn this game.'

Kieran nodded.

'Just one,' Colm said, waving a finger at his team-mate.

A few minutes later, a high ball came down on Kieran and Colm just on the edge of the D. Kieran broke it right in the path of Colm. He collected himself, dummied and then fired a rocket. Hearty saved it with an amazing diving save. Mike Frank collected the rebound and fired for goal, only for Hearty to make another incredible save with his left hand. The ball cleared the crossbar for a point. Kerry trailed by two at half-time, but the momentum was finally in their favour.

'We'll get them in the second half,' Colm said to Kieran on their way into the dressing room.

Midway through the second half, the breakthrough came. Kieran isolated himself one-on-one with Francie Bellew on the edge of the square. A high ball came in and Kieran plucked it from the sky. He dusted Bellew with a juke right out of the NBA, and then fired a laser past Hearty.

Colm jumped up in the sky as if he'd scored it himself. It was Kieran's first ever goal for Kerry.

He sprinted to celebrate with Kieran but before the ball even hit the net, Kieran was right in the face of Hearty.

'Who's the cry-baby now?' Kieran said to the goalie.

That's exactly the kind of guy Donaghy was.

There was no stopping Kerry today. Armagh fought to the bitter end, but Kerry won by eight.

The wind was in their sails and no one was questioning their bottle.

CHAPTER 26

A SECOND ALL-IRELAND TITLE

Cork were next in the All-Ireland semi-final. Kerry wanted revenge for losing the Munster final. It was their third semi-final against Cork since Colm had made his senior debut. Kerry had won their first two. Cork were a good team but everyone in the Kerry team knew they weren't the same team in Croke Park. Kerry won the semi-final by six points, 0–16 to 0–10.

It meant Colm would be the Kerry captain in the All-Ireland final.

'Your father would be so proud if he saw you lift that trophy on All-Ireland final day as captain,' his mam said.

'I know, Mam. I'll win it for him.'

Their All-Ireland opponent was familiar as well: Mayo. They'd beat Dublin in an electric semi-final. They mounted a massive comeback, and over-turned a seven-point deficit in the second half.

The Tuesday before the All-Ireland, Jack called Colm into his office.

'Colm, I have some news for you,' he said. 'I wanted to tell you first before I told any of the lads.'

'What's that, Jack?'

'I'm going to start Declan in the final. He's been flying in training. He was great against Cork as well.'

'That's brilliant,' Colm said. 'He deserves it.'

'I agree. There's just one consequence for you though,' Jack said. 'It means Declan will be restored to captain. You've been a great captain for us so I'm sorry about this. That's the tradition.'

'Oh, okay,' Colm said. He was surprised by the news.

'Now take your time to think about this, Colm. I don't want this to divide the team. I need you to be on board with this.'

Captaining your team in an All-Ireland final was such an important job. You led your team around in the parade. You collected Sam Maguire if you won.

You made the speech from the Ard Chomhairle. You appeared on the Sunday Game and were front and centre at the homecoming.

Colm would have loved the opportunity to honour his dad's memory. But Declan had been through a lot himself that summer. Colm knew how hard he had worked to get back into the Kerry starting fifteen. And Colm knew his chance as captain would eventually come.

'Declan's our captain, Jack,' Colm said. 'He has my full support.'

Everything felt so familiar for this All-Ireland final. Mayo were the opponents again. All of the players he'd soldiered with for years – the Ó Sés, Declan, Paul Galvin – were all there with him. The only thing Colm knew would be different was that his dad wouldn't be in Croke Park to watch him.

But he knew his dad would be watching from somewhere. Colm knew he had to win the All-Ireland for him.

Jack had a plan for Mayo. They'd beaten Dublin

in the semi-final after an amazing comeback, and they were riding high.

'That was their final,' Jack said in his final meeting with the team. 'This is ours.'

Mayo had brilliant forwards, but Jack knew they wouldn't have an answer for Kieran, and the havoc he'd cause.

The atmosphere during warm ups was phenomenal. It was mad when Colm thought about it: it was his fourth All-Ireland final and he was still only twenty-four. He'd played senior for Kerry for five seasons and was about to play in his fourth All-Ireland final.

The Mayo fans brought such passion and hunger. But Colm could tell their players felt an unbearable pressure to deliver a first All-Ireland since 1951.

Kerry scored the first two points of the match. The start was cagey, but the Kerry forwards could sense that the Mayo defence was there for the taking. In the seventh minute, a long diagonal ball was played into Colm around the forty-five. The instant that Colm leapt for the ball, Declan sprinted towards goal from the top of the D. Colm spotted the run, and played a hand pass that allowed to

Declan to surge into space. Declan collected the ball and spotted Kieran standing all alone in front of the goal. Declan hand passed into Kieran. As the goalie charged out, Kieran fisted right back to Declan, who had continued his run. Declan had an empty net now, and he blasted the ball into it.

Mayo were shell shocked. Now was the time to be ruthless, and Kerry went for the jugular. Moments later, Donaghy caught another highball, turned his man, and boom, a second goal for Kerry! The opening minutes were a blur, but after twelve minutes had elapsed, Gooch looked up at the scoreboard and Kerry were leading 2-4 to 0-0.

Mayo's first score was a goal in the sixteenth minute. It was one of the craziest games Colm had even played in. Anything could happen. In the twenty-sixth minute, Colm seized on a breaking ball that bounced over the Mayo backline. He juked past the keeper, but his shot at goal bounced off the post. Colm followed his shot up just like he'd learned back in Ardshanavooly. He slotted the rebound past the goalie on the near post side. Kerry led by fourteen!

'Superb skill, wonderful goal from Colm Cooper,'

the commentator on Radio Kerry shouted. 'His late father Mike would be a happy man if he were here today to see the Gooch rattle the back of the net in the All-Ireland final!'

The Kingdom's 34th All-Ireland was all but won.

When the fulltime whistle blew, Colm had scored 1-2, Donaghy had scored 1-2 and Declan had scored 1-2. It was one of the biggest routs in All-Ireland final history: 4-15 to 3-5. Amid all the joyous celebrations with his teammates and the coaching staff, Colm took a moment to look up to the sky.

'That's for you, Dad,' Colm whispered.

He then felt Declan pull his jersey.

'Come on,' he said to Colm.

'What do you mean?'

'We're lifting this trophy together.'

'What? Are you sure?'

'You captained this team as much I did. Now let's lift Sam Maguire together.'

They'd both been through so much that year. This was their moment. They climbed the steps of the Hogan Stand into the Ard Chomhairle. Declan made the speech and then the time came to raise the roofs.

'One ... two ... three,' Declan said.

And at the same moment, they lifted the Sam Maguire trophy. Colm knew that whatever happened for the rest of his career, and the rest of his life, it would be difficult to top this incredible moment.

AFTERWORD

It was a bitterly cold day in March 2017. Colm was thirty-three. Here he was, back on the beautiful wide-open field of Croke Park. He knew this might be the very last time he'd be here as a player, so he tried to remember everything.

He'd won everything in the game, bar one trophy. He was a five-time All-Ireland winner and an eight-time All-Star. In the latter stages of his intercounty career, he'd changed from a ball-winning corner forward to a visionary centre half forward. His body had changed as well. He was bigger and tougher.

The only thing Colm was missing was the same trophy he watched his brothers lift when he was just an eight-year-old: the All-Ireland club championship.

Three years earlier, Colm had torn his cruciate playing with Dr Crokes in the All-Ireland club semi-final. It was a terrible injury, and Colm wondered if he ever would really return to his best. But one of the things that motivated him most was the chance of coming back here to Croke Park, to win a club All-Ireland with his friends from Killarney.

Pat O'Shea, who Colm had worshipped as a kid in Ardshan, was the Dr Crokes bainisteoir now.

The Dr Crokes team was full of young lads whom Colm had mentored when they were U12s. These guys were like his extended family. Winning All-Ireland's with Kerry was amazing, but there was nothing in the GAA quite like this.

Colm was still technically a Kerry intercounty player and many people were wondering if he'd rejoin the panel after the match.

'Will you retire from Kerry if ye win today, Gooch?' a steward had asked when the Dr Crokes team arrived in the stadium.

Colm shrugged his shoulders. He wasn't sure himself. His only focus was winning this one match with Dr Crokes.

Their opposition was Slaughtneil from Derry. They were a tough team with tremendous spirit. But

Colm knew it would be Dr Crokes' day. Slaught-neil scored an early goal, but Colm answered back with a goal of his own to calm the nerves of his teammates. It was a fierce game played on a cold Dublin evening. Dr Crokes lead 1-9 to 1-7 deep into second half added time. Colm was taking a sideline kick deep in his own half as the Dr Crokes supporters whistled at the ref.

'Blow it up,' they shouted.

When Colm started playing football, a forward like him never would have dropped so deep but football had changed over his career. It was seventeen years since he broke through in the Dr Crokes senior – a lot had changed in Gaelic football!

Colm kicked the ball in and a second later, the ref blew the whistle for full time.

'YES!' Colm shouted. He ran right for the Kerry sideline and jumped right into the arms of his manager and friend Pat. They fell over on the ground as photographers surrounded them and all their selectors and teammates jumped on top of them.

He'd experienced everything in football, but he'd never known happiness quite like this. Winning an All-Ireland with your friends and neighbours was the greatest feeling in the GAA. He met his brothers and sisters at bottom of the Hogan Stand. They hugged and cried.

The celebrations would go on for a few days in Killarney, and a few weeks later, Colm would announce his retirement from intercounty football. He'd achieved everything he could have ever dreamed of in the GAA, and so much more. Some people said he was the best Kerry forward of all time. Some said he was the best player of all time.

Not bad for a freckly redhead from Ardshanavooly.

COLM COOPER'S ACHIEVEMENTS

Championship appearances with Kerry – 85

Total Championship score: 23-283
  (Kerry's all-time leading Championship scorer)

5-time All-Ireland winner with Kerry
  (2004, 2006, 2007, 2009, 2014)

9-time Munster Champion with Kerry

8-time All-Star

Club All-Ireland winner with Dr Crokes – 2017

Selected for International Rules team – 2005

GREAT IRISH SPORTS STARS

ALSO AVAILABLE

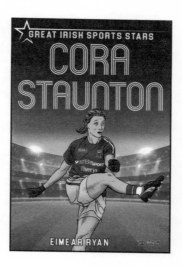

A Gaelic football hero in Mayo, a trailblazer in Aussie Rules
Winner of FOUR All-Irelands + ELEVEN All-Stars

The story of how a football-mad girl
became a living legend.